TERROR BY NIGHT

TERROR BY NIGHT

TERRY CAFFEY with JAMES H. PENCE

The true story of the brutal Texas murder that destroyed a family, restored one man's faith, and shocked a nation

TYNDALE HOUSE PUBLISHERS, INC.
CAROL STREAM, ILLINOIS

Visit Tyndale online at www.tyndale.com.

Visit Terry Caffey's website at http://terrycaffey.com.

Visit James Pence's website at http://jamespence.com.

TYNDALE and Tyndale's quill logo are registered trademarks of Tyndale House Publishers, Inc.

Terror by Night: The True Story of the Brutal Texas Murder That Destroyed a Family, Restored One Man's Faith, and Shocked a Nation

Designed by Stephen Vosloo

Edited by Susan Taylor

Published in association with the literary agency of WordServe Literary Group, Ltd., 10152 S. Knoll Circle, Highlands Ranch, CO 80130.

Unless otherwise indicated, all Scripture quotations are taken from the New American Standard Bible,® copyright © 1960, 1962, 1963, 1968, 1971, 1972, 1973, 1975, 1977, 1995 by The Lockman Foundation. Used by permission.

Scripture quotations marked NIV are taken from the Holy Bible, *New International Version,*® *NIV.*® Copyright © 1973, 1978, 1984 by Biblica, Inc.™ Used by permission of Zondervan. All rights reserved worldwide. www.zondervan.com.

Scripture quotations marked NKJV are taken from the New King James Version.® Copyright © 1982 by Thomas Nelson, Inc. Used by permission. All rights reserved. *NKJV* is a trademark of Thomas Nelson, Inc.

Scripture quotations marked KJV are taken from the *Holy Bible*, King James Version.

Library of Congress Cataloging-in-Publication Data

Caffey, Terry.
    Terror by night : the true story of the brutal Texas murder that destroyed a family, restored one man's faith, and shocked a nation / Terry Caffey ; with James H. Pence.
        p. cm.
    ISBN 978-1-4143-3476-9 (hc)
    1. Consolation. 2. Suffering—Religious aspects—Christianity. 3. Murder—Religious aspects—Christianity. 4. Murder—Texas. 5. Caffey, Terry. I. Pence, James H. II. Title.
    BV4909.C34 2009
    364.152'3092—dc22
    [B]   2009028694

ISBN 978-1-4143-7965-4 Softcover

Printed in the United States of America

18 17 16 15 14 13 12
7   6   5   4   3   2   1

A12005 998257

To Penny, Bubba, and Tyler

To Michelle Lynn Pence (6/1/87–6/8/87)
and
Elaina Michelle Pence (6/10/09)

God, in His sovereign grace and wisdom, took our first child,
Michelle Lynn, on June 8, 1987, when she was one week old.

Almost exactly twenty-two years later—just as I was finishing this
book—He gave us our first grandchild, Elaina Michelle.

Our God is a God who restores.

CONTENTS

Terry's Acknowledgments

I want to thank my church, Miracle Faith Baptist, and the communities of Emory and Alba for all your prayers and support. I couldn't have made it without you.

To Tommy and Helen (Paw and Maw) Gaston: Thank you for all your love and support for Penny and the kids down through the years.

Brother Andy Russell of Martin Baptist Church in New Albany, Mississippi, you have been my brother in Christ, mentor, and friend. Thanks for giving me the boost that I needed in my ministry.

Many thanks to Rodney Gipson and family for all you have done. Our fishing trip in May of 2008 changed my life. You have been there for me when so many were nowhere to be found. Thanks for listening when I needed an ear.

No words can express my love for you, Brother Terry Dowty. You have become the brother that I never had. Thank you for being there so many times when I needed a friend, even at three in the morning.

I want to thank Penny's parents, Larry and Virginia Daily. We have been through so much together, and by God's grace we will carry on. You raised a wonderful daughter, and it showed by her devotion to me and her love for our children. I'll always be thankful for the years we all shared together.

Last, but certainly not least, I want to thank my new family: Sonja, Blake, and Tanner. I couldn't imagine going through this without your love and support. You have seen me through so much. You have helped me realize what it means to love again. You were there as I spent long hours and reopened many wounds while working on this project. For that I will be eternally grateful.

James's Acknowledgments

The longer I write, the better I understand that, while mine is a solitary profession, I would never be able to bring a project to completion without the help of countless others.

Thanks to my agent, Greg Johnson, for doing a great job in representing both Terry and me, and for all your hard work in finding a home for *Terror by Night*.

Thanks to Carol Traver and all at Tyndale for working so hard to produce *Terror by Night* in record time.

During the writing process, I had to step back from my Karate for Homeschoolers classes in order to have more time to write. A special thanks to my wife, Laurel, and my daughter Charlene for taking over the administrative duties. Also thanks to my black-belt assistant instructors: Glen Dempsey and Ruger Carstens, and to the brown belts who helped them: Alec Barrett, Gary Casey, Joseph Lostritto, Rachelle Lostritto, and Hannah McKinney. The classes didn't miss a beat, and I have you all to thank. You did an awesome job.

To my mentor, Cec Murphey: Thanks for believing in me and for challenging me to grow as a writer.

To my wife, Laurel: Thanks for being my number one encourager, first reader, and editor. I couldn't do it without you.

Thanks to everyone who prayed for Terry and me while this project was ongoing. Your prayers were a constant source of encouragement.

Finally, thanks to Terry Caffey for choosing me to help you write your story. I've had the joy of knowing both of your families, and it was a great privilege for me to be a part of this project.

Introduction

You have delivered my soul from death,
My eyes from tears,
And my feet from falling.
I will walk before the LORD
In the land of the living.
—PSALM 116:8-9 (NKJV)

AFTER I LOST my precious wife and family, along with everything I owned, the last thing I wanted to hear was that God would work all things together for good because I loved Him and was called according to His purpose. I wasn't angry with God. Not at first, anyway. But I did feel like He'd abandoned me. In the weeks following the brutal murders of my wife, Penny, and my two sons, Matthew and Tyler, and the arrest of my daughter, Erin, I entered into a time of spiritual and emotional darkness that I wouldn't have dreamed possible only a few months before. I felt as if the doors of heaven were shut and God was the One who'd closed them.

I couldn't understand that. I had dedicated my life to serving Him.

Despite some struggles with our daughter Erin and her choice of boyfriends, Penny and I had entered into 2008 very optimistic about the future. Soon after we were married in 1989, we'd started working with the youth in our church. That continued when we were at

Miracle Faith Baptist Church several years later. During that time, I sensed God calling me to a broader ministry. I did some pulpit supply for local pastors, and the more I preached the more I felt that God wanted me to move in this direction. After I'd been preaching for several years, my church made plans to formally ordain me for ministry. They set the time of my ordination for April 2008. I still wasn't sure if I was going to be a pastor or an evangelist. All I knew was that I intended to serve God.

I wanted my family to serve Him, too. When we moved out to our twelve-acre property in Alba, Texas, our neighbor and dear friend Tommy Gaston presented us with a split cedar log. On it, he'd inscribed our family name, "The Caffeys," in large letters. Below that, he added the Bible reference Joshua 24:15.

I knew the verse well. "As for me and my house, we will serve the LORD." I love that Scripture verse because in it, Joshua took a stand on serving God. I felt that since God took a stand for us when Jesus died on the cross, my family and I would also take our stand for Him.

But in the aftermath of March 1, 2008—my personal 9/11—I didn't understand what was happening. I'd taken my stand for God, but God had allowed something terrible to happen to my family. Where was He? Had He turned His back on us? Had He forgotten us?

I felt like the writer of Psalm 88:

I suffer Your terrors; I am overcome.
Your burning anger has passed over me;
Your terrors have destroyed me.
They have surrounded me like water all day long;
They have encompassed me altogether.
You have removed lover and friend far from me;
My acquaintances are in darkness.
—PSALM 88:15-18

I wandered in a black fog that offered no hint of clearing. And there I would have remained, were it not for the gracious hand of God.

Some may wonder why I'd want to write a book about what happened to me. To be honest, there were times during the process that I wondered that myself. As I worked through the various chapters of *Terror by Night*, I dredged up memories, thoughts, and experiences that I would have preferred to leave buried. There were times when I simply had to stop working and cry for a while. It would have been very easy to quit. Nevertheless, I wrote this book, not because I wanted to, but because I had to.

Terror by Night is not about my loss and personal tragedy; it is about God's faithfulness. I walked through horror so great I can't imagine anyone else living through it, let alone me. But all the time, God was there. I did not always sense His presence, especially not at the beginning. At times I didn't even want His presence. And, yes, there was a period when I became angry at His silence. I'm not proud of it, and I'm not saying it was right to feel that way. But that's how I felt.

And yet as I faced profound loss, God never left my side. As I look back, I can see His hand in everything that happened. And I have dedicated the rest of my life to sharing with others how God has used this tragedy to bring about good.

I know that by writing this book, I open myself to the charge of trying to profit from my tragedy. God knows my heart. That is the farthest thing from my mind. I have no desire to profit from my family's deaths. I'd give anything to have them back. I wrote *Terror by Night* so that God would be glorified and so that those who read it would understand that no matter what comes into their lives, God still cares. I want everyone to know that God loves them and that even in the worst tragedies they can trust Him, because He has everything under control.

Finally, I want this book to be Penny, Matthew, and Tyler's legacy. Their lives were cut short in a terrible tragedy, but through *Terror by*

Night, they will continue to have an impact in this world for Jesus Christ. To borrow from the author of the New Testament book of Hebrews, "Even though they are dead, they still speak."

—Terry Caffey

CHAPTER 1

A GATHERING STORM

You will not be afraid of the terror by night,
Or of the arrow that flies by day. —PSALM 91:5

THE DAY MY WORLD started to collapse was about as pretty as they come. The sun shone in a crystal clear, blue sky, and the air had just enough nip in it to remind you that it was February. North Texas winters are unpredictable at best. One day you might scramble to keep your car from sliding off an icy highway, and the next day lounge around in shorts and a T-shirt. This wasn't a shorts-and-T-shirt day, but it was beautiful all the same.

Around 10:30 a.m. on February 20, I pulled my van into the parking lot of King Place Apartments to check on my father. He had just been released from the hospital a few days before, and I wanted to see if he needed anything.

My sister and I had moved him to Greenville, Texas, from his home in Garland the previous year. He had been struggling with diabetes and heart trouble for several years, and it was not unusual for us to receive several emergency calls a month. This meant we drove an hour and a half from Alba to Dallas each time he called 911. When the emergencies became more and more frequent, my sister Mary and I had finally sat him down and told him that he had to move closer.

I wanted him to move to Emory, a small town of about twelve hundred only a few minutes from Penny and me, but he dug in his heels.

"Emory is too small. There won't be anything for me to do there."

I understood. After living his whole life on the outskirts of Dallas, my dad thought a move to a rural farming community was too much to ask. Greenville became our compromise. It was about halfway between Emory and Garland and shortened any emergency drives to about forty minutes. Its population of about twenty-five thousand was more suitable to my dad. True, it wasn't Garland or Dallas, but at least there would be things for him to do. And because I worked in Greenville, I could check on him regularly.

This day, he didn't answer when I rang the doorbell.

I knocked on the door and waited. Still no response. I wasn't particularly worried. Daddy had made some friends in the months since he'd moved to Greenville. Maybe one of his buddies had picked him up and taken him out to coffee at the Royal Drive-In, a local Dairy Queen clone and a regular hangout for many of Greenville's senior citizens.

I decided to make a few more deliveries and check on him later.

But when I stopped by again after lunch and still couldn't get a response, I knew something was wrong.

"Daddy, are you okay?" I called his name and knocked again.

Then I pounded.

No answer.

Fear welled up inside me as I walked around to the back of the building. I tried the sliding glass door, but the metal burglar bar was still in the track. I cupped my hands around my eyes and peered through the glass but couldn't see my father anywhere.

I had to get in there.

I went around to the front and used my spare key to unlock the door, but the metal security chain kept the door from opening more than a few inches.

"Daddy? Clarence?" I called through the crack.

Silence.

Finally, I kicked the door in. Fear gave way to panic as I ran through the apartment, calling his name.

I found him lying facedown in his bedroom. My throat tightened as I crouched down and touched his hand. I checked his wrist for a pulse but knew I wouldn't find one. His body was already cold.

That was the first time I had ever seen a dead body that wasn't in a funeral home.

At first I fought back the tears. I'm not sure why. Maybe I felt the need to be "strong" or "responsible" because I was the one who found him. But this was my dad. And as the reality of his death began to sink in, I gave in and let my tears flow.

Daddy had suffered so many health problems over the past few years that on some level I think I knew his death was coming. But that didn't make it any easier when the time came. It just hurt so much, especially because it had happened so suddenly. I cried not only for the loss of my dad but also because I didn't get a chance to say good-bye, to say all the things a son needs to say to the father he loves before they part for the last time.

My one comforting thought in those moments was that I knew where my daddy was. He loved the Lord and had trusted Jesus Christ as his Savior many years before. I knew without a doubt that one day I would see him again.

I pulled out my cell phone and called 911. Then I called my wife, Penny. She had loved Dad, too, and needed to know that he was gone.

UNPLANNED EXPENSES

Even though funerals can be expensive, you don't really think about the expense when you lose loved ones. You want to show one last time how much you cared about them and how much you will miss them. You want them to have a nice funeral. It's not too much to ask.

We knew that my father had a small life-insurance policy that would cover his funeral costs, so we weren't worried about money. But when we met with the funeral director, we learned that my father had cashed in the policy without telling any of the family. There was no money to pay for his funeral.

Penny and I walked past a line of expensive caskets costing thousands of dollars each. We weren't poor, but we had only a few thousand dollars in savings. I felt a twinge of guilt as I said, "Could you show us the least expensive one you've got?"

The funeral director smiled and told us that he understood. He showed us a casket that cost only fifteen hundred dollars. But a service at the funeral home and the burial would be two thousand more.

"We can't afford that. Can't you go any cheaper?" I said, now feeling really guilty.

We spent some time looking at different options and finally got the price down to eight hundred for the casket and fifteen hundred for a direct burial with no graveside service. We would also hold the funeral at a church rather than at the funeral home.

Penny and I cleaned out our already small savings account to pay for my father's funeral.

CLEANING OUT THE APARTMENT

The rest of the week was a whirlwind of activity. My dad had been on a month-to-month lease at King Place, because he was thinking about moving to a different complex. Unfortunately, that meant we had only a week to clean out his apartment. Otherwise we'd have to pay another month's rent, and we didn't have the money for that.

So in addition to preparing for a memorial service, we had to clean the apartment, pack my dad's things, and try to sell them. We decided to hold an estate sale at the apartment on Saturday, the day before the service.

To say it was chaos at my dad's apartment that day would be a gross understatement. My sisters, Mary and Tina, along with Tina's three grown children, assisted Penny and me as we sorted through all my father's belongings, kept what we wanted, priced what we didn't want, set the items out for the sale—which was running at the same time—and cleaned the apartment room by room. To complicate matters, all of our children were there. Between our three, Mary's two girls, and Tina and her children, not to mention the people who'd come for the sale, it was standing room only in that little apartment. You could hardly move. That's why we were delighted when Penny's sister, Mandy, stopped by to see if she could help. When she saw the children running in and out of the apartment, she offered the perfect solution.

"Why don't I just take the kids over to my place for the day?" she asked.

Mandy lived in Greenville, so the kids wouldn't be too far away. And it would definitely make it easier for us to get our work done. We all agreed that this would be a huge help, so Mandy piled the kids into her car and took them to her house until we were finished with the sale.

I had no idea then, but that decision set in motion a downward spiral of events that would ultimately lead to the murders of my family.

THE FUNERAL

We held my father's memorial service on Sunday, February 24, at Grace Baptist Church in Garland, my father's church. He'd maintained his membership there even after he moved to Greenville. Because we had paid for a direct burial, there was no casket or viewing. Dad had been buried a day earlier at Williams Cemetery in Garland, in a plot beside my mother. For the memorial service, we set a few pictures of Dad on the Communion table. About 150 people filled the little redbrick church building.

Musically, it was a family affair. Music had always been an important part of our household. Penny was a member of the Southern gospel group called The Gaston Family Singers, and she could play gospel piano with the best of them. The children loved to hear her, and the sound of her piano filled our house daily. One of our favorite family activities was to stand around the piano and sing while Penny played.

As the service began, Penny played, and our sixteen-year-old daughter, Erin, sang "Come Morning" and "I Want to Stroll over Heaven with You." Later, my thirteen-year-old son, Matthew, and I played "Amazing Grace" on harmonica, and then my niece Courtney sang. Tyler, only eight, didn't take part in the service. He was too shy.

Pastor Allison brought a message from the Twenty-third Psalm. I don't remember many of the details; everything was such a blur. I do remember that he told some good stories about my dad. The service wasn't fancy, but it was a fitting tribute to a fine man. I went home that day sad but also happy that my dad was not suffering any longer and that he was in a better place.

• • •

When a funeral is over, it's time to slowly begin to adjust to a new life, a life without the person you've lost. But I had no time to adjust. No time to grieve. I took the next few days off and spent much of the next week wrapping up the details of my father's life: turning off utilities, stopping his cable service, closing out his bank account. It was a stressful time, but at that moment I had no idea it was only the beginning. I didn't know it then, but my father's death was like the dark sky before a tornado. Soon a storm would blow through my life and leave devastation behind it.

One week to the day after my dad's funeral, Penny, Matthew, and Tyler would be dead. I would be in the ICU, fighting for my life.

And Erin would be in jail, charged with three counts of capital murder.

CHAPTER 2

CHARLIE

*"Simon, Simon, behold, Satan has demanded permission
to sift you like wheat; but I have prayed for you, that
your faith may not fail; and you, when once you have
turned again, strengthen your brothers."*
—JESUS, LUKE 22:31-32

LOSING MY FATHER, having to drain our savings to pay for his funeral,
and having to empty his apartment so quickly were all stressful situ-
ations. But they were intensified by our concern over Erin's relationship with Charlie Wilkinson.

Charlie hovered like a dark cloud over everything else that week.

Erin had been working at the Emory Sonic drive-in for several
months when she came home one September afternoon and told
us that she had met the most wonderful guy named Charlie. Penny

and I rolled our eyes and held our breath. Up to this point, Erin's track record in choosing boyfriends had not been very good. She had been dating for only a few months, but so far she had gravitated toward boys we considered to be troublemakers or rebels. She also preferred boys who were not Christians. When Penny and I spoke to her about that, she simply answered, "I can witness to them."

The problem was, it didn't usually work out that way. The boys Erin dated would even swear around us and around the church youth leaders. If Erin was trying to be a positive influence in these boys' lives, it didn't seem to be working.

So, naturally, I was anxious to meet Charlie. Maybe he would be different.

To say that our first meeting did not go well would be an understatement.

It was a pleasant October evening when I pulled into our driveway and walked in the front door. Penny was in the kitchen getting supper ready. Matthew and Tyler were sitting on the couch watching SpongeBob. Erin was setting the table.

And there was Charlie. He sat sideways in my recliner, hanging his legs over the arm.

"You must be Charlie," I said.

He glanced up from the TV and replied, "And you are?"

I stiffened. Maybe I'm old-fashioned, but I believe that a young person should be respectful when speaking to an adult.

"Do you always sit like that?" I asked.

"Yeah," he said, looking back at the TV.

I replied, "Not in my chair, you don't. Why don't you stand up and greet me like a man?"

After a few seconds, he stood up and gave me a weak handshake, looking off to the side and chomping on his chewing gum.

I walked over to Penny at the sink and whispered, "I'm not sure I like this guy."

She smiled up at me and said, "Oh, well. You know how kids can be these days."

All I could think was, *This guy wants to go out with my daughter?*

Later that evening, Penny and I discussed Charlie as we sat together in bed.

"He seems nice and all." said Penny.

"Sweetheart," I replied, "he's eighteen. He's a grown man. Erin's barely sixteen."

"He's still in high school," said Penny. "Let's just keep an eye on things and see how it goes. He's probably harmless."

"What he is, is disrespectful," I said.

I didn't think he was harmless. I thought I could see right through him. And I didn't like what I saw.

GROWING CONCERNS

I didn't like Charlie, but I was willing to go along with what Penny wanted. She thought he was kind of cute, although a bit of a know-it-all. Whenever adults were engaged in a conversation and Charlie was in the room, he was always quick to interrupt. And it didn't matter what the topic was; Charlie always knew everything there was to know about it.

As the weeks passed, he came over to our house more frequently. Eventually, he became a regular fixture. Penny was gracious and patient; that was just her way. But it wasn't long before she began to have questions of her own.

Penny had homeschooled the children for several years, but at the beginning of the 2007–2008 school year, Matthew and Tyler decided to go back to public school. Because Erin had a day job at Sonic, she decided to continue with homeschooling. However, about midway through the fall semester, she changed her mind and decided that she wanted to start public school again. We didn't make the connection at the time, but later we suspected that Charlie was the reason for Erin's decision. By going to public school, she could be with Charlie more, and without our supervision.

As time passed, Penny's concerns grew. One evening, she was getting supper ready. Charlie sat at the dining-room table, talking and getting in the way, while Penny and Erin tried to get the food prepared and the table set. Finally, Penny had had enough.

"Charlie," she said, "don't sit there in the way. If you're not going to help, go watch TV or do something else."

I was outside working in my shed. Charlie came out to see me, but we were like oil and water. Things were always tense when we were together. I didn't know how to deal with Charlie. I didn't want him dating my daughter, and I didn't hide that fact. So he didn't stay out there with me very long.

A little while later, Penny walked toward the bathroom and noticed the door was open a crack. She pushed it open, thinking no one was in there. Instead, she found Charlie going through the medicine cabinet.

"What are you doing?" she asked.

Charlie scrambled for an answer. "I'm trying to find some ibuprofen. I have a headache."

Irritated, Penny said, "You shouldn't be going through people's things without permission. If you need something for a headache, ask first."

When Penny told me about this, I confronted Charlie: "There are boundaries in people's houses," I said. "You need to ask if you need medicine. Don't just go through our cabinets."

Our talk didn't help. A week later I found him doing exactly the same thing. I told him again that he shouldn't go through our things without asking.

By this time, both Penny and I knew we needed to keep an eye on him.

GIFTS

December went by smoothly, but not long after the holidays, things took a turn for the worse. Charlie began showering Erin with gifts. She came home regularly with roses, candy, and cheap jewelry. Penny and I couldn't figure out where the money was coming from because Charlie didn't have a job. We asked Erin, and she told us she didn't know.

One day early in January, Erin was going around and showing everyone in church a new ring Charlie had given her. One of the kids in the youth group came up to Penny. "Have you seen Erin's new ring?" she asked.

Penny said no and then went looking for Erin. Along the way she found me and told me what she had heard. Together, we went looking for Erin. We found her talking to some other girls and asked her to show us the ring.

This was no piece of cheap jewelry; it was an expensive wedding ring.

"Where is Charlie?" I asked.

"Outside playing basketball," said Erin.

"You two stay here," I said.

I took a deep breath, trying to maintain control as I went out to talk to Charlie. He was on the basketball court, shooting hoops with a group of other boys.

"Charlie," I called.

He looked at me—then started running toward me. Even though it was cool outside, he was all sweaty from playing basketball.

"Yeah," he said, "what do you want?"

That was the wrong thing to say. I was already agitated over his giving Erin the ring, and his attitude just made me angrier.

I showed him the ring. "What does this mean?"

"It's just a friendship ring," he said.

"It looks like an expensive wedding ring. Where did you get it?"

"It was my mother's."

"But what does it mean?" I asked again.

Charlie looked upset. "It just means that I'm promising myself to her."

"It's a very inappropriate gift," I said. "Do you realize that Erin is only sixteen years old?"

Charlie rolled his eyes and said, "Yeah, Terry, I know."

I was tired of his disrespectful attitude. "From now on, you will address me with 'Yes, sir, Mr. Caffey,' not 'Yeah, Terry.' Tomorrow, you need to come over to the house. Penny and I want to talk to you and Erin."

Charlie showed up the next afternoon, just as we'd asked. When he arrived, Penny was in the kitchen, and Matthew and Tyler were in the living room. Erin was upstairs in her room.

When I heard Charlie pull into the driveway, I said, "Boys, go upstairs to your rooms for a while. And tell Erin to come down."

Erin came down, and I could tell by the look on her face that she was worried. We sat them both down on the couch, and I took out the ring and handed it back to Charlie.

"We're laying down some new rules," I said. "Charlie, you've been coming over here practically every night of the week, and that's going to stop. You see each other at school every day, so you don't need to be over here every night. From now on, you can come over one day a week, and you have to leave by nine o'clock. Not nine fifteen or nine thirty, the way you have been."

Erin and Charlie's response was subdued, but they appeared to accept our terms.

After that confrontation, we all hoped things would get better. But Penny and I still were worried and prayed often about their relationship. Erin and Charlie seemed to want to take it right to the edge.

Maybe we should have forced Erin to break up with Charlie then.

CHANGES

Right around the time of the ring incident, in January and February of 2008, we noticed visible changes in Erin. She had always been careful about her appearance. She had never left the house looking less than perfect. Her hair, makeup, and clothes always had to be just right, and she'd get up early to make sure she looked good before she left for school. Now she stopped wearing makeup and quit fussing with her hair. Her clothing choices were poor too. Before, she was practically a walking fashion statement. Now she looked as if she just picked clothes at random, without caring whether they matched or looked good together.

And it wasn't just the change in Erin's appearance that worried us. Her attitude was changing too. Before, she had always been a sweet, soft-spoken girl, but now she had begun to show attitude when speaking with Penny and me.

Erin and Penny had always gotten along well, but now there were times when I'd come home and find Penny crying because of something Erin had said. One day Erin cut Penny deeply when she said, "You know, I can leave here when I'm seventeen."

When Penny told me that, I said, "If she wants to leave when she's seventeen, I won't stand in her way."

"No," said Penny, still crying. "Don't tell her that."

"Honey," I said, "Erin has to understand that she has two younger siblings in this house. And I'm not going to let her disrupt their lives. If she's that unhappy, I'll let her go."

I went up to Erin's room and sat down beside her.

"So I hear you want to leave here when you're seventeen," I said.

Erin nodded.

"You're going to have bills. You'll need an apartment. Who's going to take care of all that?"

Her voice was soft, almost childlike. "Charlie."

"Charlie?" I said. "Charlie doesn't have a job. He can't even take care of himself. How's he going to do that?"

Erin just shrugged.

"Look," I said. "If you're that unhappy here, I won't stand in your way. When you're seventeen, you can go. But you need to understand that this house doesn't have a revolving door. You're not going to go out and party and live it up, come back six months later and stir things up here, and then go again. If you leave, you leave. I'll always love you," I said, "but I've got to think of Matthew and Tyler, too. I'm not going to allow you to disrupt their lives just because you think you've got to have your own way."

I didn't believe there was much danger that Erin would leave home to be with Charlie. I just thought that was the kind of thing teenagers say when they want to leverage a little more freedom from their parents. Charlie couldn't take care of Erin, and she knew it.

MYSPACE

On Wednesday, February 27, only three days after my father's funeral, my cell phone rang. It was Penny. Her voice was strained.

"Can you get off work a little early and meet me at the library?"

"Penny, I've been off work almost a week. I really can't afford to take off early. Can't it wait until I get home?" I asked.

Penny began to cry. "No, it can't. I need to show you something."

Whatever it was, I could tell it was serious, so I agreed to meet her at the library shortly before it closed. I found out then that Penny's sister, Mandy, had called her with some disturbing news.

Because we didn't have a computer, the kids would usually get on the Internet at Mandy's or at the library. While Erin was at Mandy's during the apartment sale, she got on Charlie's MySpace page. But when she left, she forgot to log out. Mandy was aware of our concern about Erin and Charlie's relationship, and when she saw Charlie's page, she knew she had to talk to us. She didn't tell us at first, because she knew we had our hands full with the memorial service and cleaning out the apartment. It wasn't until that Wednesday that she remembered to mention it to Penny.

Penny met me at the library's front door. The minute I saw her, I knew something was seriously wrong.

"What's the matter?" I asked.

"Mandy showed me Charlie's MySpace page. You need to see this."

We entered the library and went to the computer tables. Penny sat down at the terminal and brought up Charlie's page. The instant I saw it, I felt my face flush.

"How can Erin even like someone like this?" I asked.

Penny just shook her head.

Charlie's page was filled with references to drinking and sex. One person had posted a message telling Charlie to bring his b---- of a girlfriend over for the weekend so they could get drunk and have sex.

What was on that page was the exact opposite of everything we believed in, everything we had ever taught Erin. I couldn't understand it. Erin had always been a good kid who made good choices. But it seemed that over the last six months all of that had gone out the window.

"He's going to take Erin down with him," Penny said.

"No, he's not," I replied. "We're putting a stop to this today."

CONFRONTATION

That evening, after supper and before church, I asked the boys to go up to their rooms for a little while.

"Erin," I said, "we need to talk to you."

She sat down on the couch, and we sat in our chairs, opposite her. "We looked at Charlie's MySpace page today," I said.

Erin looked at the floor.

"It's filled with profanity and four-letter words. There are liquor bottles on it. They're talking about getting drunk and having sex. Erin, you weren't raised like that. Your mother and I have tried to give you some room to make your own decisions, but that's over now, at least where Charlie is concerned. We know you like this boy, but what we saw on his MySpace page goes against what we believe is best for you and everything we have ever taught you. When you're eighteen, you can make your own decisions about the guys you run around with, but for now, we're still in charge. This relationship ends today."

I wasn't sure what kind of reaction I had expected. Erin had grown very disrespectful and smart-mouthed lately. But she didn't blow up or spout off at us. Instead, tears filled Erin's eyes, and she started to cry.

"I've wanted to break up with Charlie for a while, but I just don't know how to do it."

"Just tell him it's over," I said. "Blame it on us if you want to. You can do it tonight at church," I said. "Just be sure that you do it in a public place, like the church parking lot. That way there will be other people around."

Erin nodded.

"You'd better go up and finish getting ready for church," I said.

After Erin went upstairs to her bedroom, I put my arm around Penny. A sense of relief washed over both of us. It had been a rocky six months since Charlie had entered our lives, and both Penny and I were ready for it to be over. We hoped that at last our lives could get back to normal.

PHONE CALL

I didn't go to church with my family that night. Between the stress of losing my dad and everything we'd gone through with Erin and Charlie, I just wanted to be alone and rest. As I sat in my recliner, watching TV and enjoying the peace and quiet, the phone rang. It was our church's youth director.

"Mr. Caffey, this is Sarah. Is Penny there?"

"They haven't gotten home yet, Sarah. Can I help you?"

"I just wanted to check and see if they were okay. Erin just broke up with Charlie, and they both seemed to be pretty upset. Charlie spun out of the church parking lot."

"Thanks for letting me know, Sarah. I'll keep an eye out for them."

It wasn't long before Penny's van pulled into the driveway. When they came into the house, Erin stormed up to her room without saying a word.

After the boys went to their rooms to get ready for bed, I told Penny about Sarah's call and asked what was going on.

"Sarah told me that she heard someone peeling out of the church parking lot. She went outside to see what the commotion was and learned that it was Charlie. He was really mad. I was embarrassed by what he did."

"Well, I'm glad it's over," I said.

I went upstairs and knocked on Erin's door.

"Come in," she said.

I opened the door and poked my head in. "You okay?"

She looked up at me. "I'll be fine."

I could see from her red eyes that she'd been crying.

I went in and sat down beside her on her bed. "I know that was hard to do," I said, trying to find some words of comfort for Erin. "It may not seem like it now, but it'll all blow over in time. He's not the only boy in the world."

Erin nodded.

I kissed her good night and went back downstairs.

"How's she doing?" Penny asked.

"She's upset, but I think she'll be okay."

Penny and I sat up in bed, talking for a long time about Erin and Charlie, the loss of my dad, and everything else that had been going on lately. The general consensus was that we were glad it was all over.

"It's been quite a storm, hasn't it?" Penny said.

"Yeah, but it's over now."

I had no idea the storm was only beginning.

CHAPTER 3

THE LAST GOOD TIMES

Every good thing given and every perfect gift is from above,
coming down from the Father of lights, with whom there is
no variation or shifting shadow. —JAMES 1:17

WHEN I WENT to work on Thursday, I felt as if a ten-ton weight had been lifted from my shoulders. Erin had been dating Charlie for only a few months, but it had felt like years. I hadn't realized how stressed we'd all been until that tension was removed. For the first time in months, it felt as if the clouds had lifted and the sun was shining again.

Penny and I talked it over and decided that maybe we all needed a little getaway to help us forget the difficulties of the past few weeks, and we knew just the place. We decided to surprise the kids with the news that evening.

We were all in our pj's, sitting around the dining-room table and playing a game of SKIP-BO. It had been a pleasant evening.

"Kids," Penny said, "we've got a surprise for you."

"What is it?" asked Tyler, his blue eyes sparkling.

"Well," she continued, "we're overdue for a family trip, and we thought it might be nice to get away for a few days next weekend."

"Where?" asked Matthew.

Penny and I flashed each other a knowing grin.

"Arkansas," I said.

The kids whooped in delight. They all knew exactly where in Arkansas I meant. Our favorite family getaway was Petit Jean State Park, northwest of Little Rock. We'd visited the park several times, and the children loved going there.

Overlooking Cedar Creek Canyon, Petit Jean Mountain had a mystique all its own. The park took its name from the legend of Petit Jean ("Little John"), the nickname given to a young woman whose fiancé had been commissioned by the French government to explore the Louisiana Territory. Not wanting to be separated from her love, she cut her hair, disguised herself as a cabin boy, and joined the expedition. The sailors nicknamed her Petit Jean. She survived the Atlantic crossing and traveled with the explorers. Eventually, Petit Jean became gravely ill. On her deathbed, she revealed her identity to her fiancé and asked to be buried on the mountain she had come to love.

We didn't know whether or not the legend was true; we loved the place for its sheer beauty.

"Can we hike down the canyon trail again?" Matthew asked.

"Sure," I said.

"Mama will have to be more careful this time," Tyler added, giggling.

One of our favorite things to do there was to hike to the bottom of Cedar Creek Canyon, where Cedar Falls comes crashing down ninety-five feet into a serene pool. It's a tough hike, and the last time we went down, Penny slipped on some wet rocks and fell.

"Can we stop in Hot Springs, too?" Erin asked. She and Penny loved shopping in the little shops on the strip.

"We can go to Hot Springs," I said. "But we'd better make sure Matthew remembers his luggage this time."

The kids laughed. On a previous trip to Hot Springs, we were unloading our luggage in the motel parking lot when Matthew asked, "Where's mine?"

He had packed his suitcase but forgot to load it in the car. It sat at home, more than five hours away. He started to cry, but we told him it would be okay. We'd just go to Wal-Mart and get him what he needed for the trip. That was a costly vacation, but it was well worth it. We all laughed about it later.

Our game of SKIP-BO went on, and I felt as if all of us were on the same page for the first time in months.

A HEAVEN-SENT OPPORTUNITY

Our family trip to Arkansas would have to wait a week because I was on emergency call that weekend. My job with Praxair often required me to cover large distances, setting up hospital beds or installing oxygen concentrators in patients' homes. I also had to make "death calls," which meant picking up equipment after a patient had died. I spent much of my day driving from one location to another, often lifting heavy equipment into and out of my van.

I enjoyed my work, but it was physically demanding and tiring. And although we were able to make ends meet on my salary, we had to stay on a pretty strict budget. There wasn't much left over for savings or extras. That's why we felt that God was pouring out blessings when Penny called me that morning.

"Terry, a man named Ben Draper from The Henry Group in

Greenville just called. He wants to know if you'd come in for a job interview."

The Henry Group has a small factory just outside Greenville where they make industrial ovens. I'd put in a résumé there more than two years earlier but had never heard anything in response. I had long since forgotten about it.

"You're kidding," I said.

"No. He told me that your résumé kept popping up on his desk and he felt that God wanted him to talk to you. Do you think you could get over to see him?"

"When does he want me to come?"

"About three," Penny said.

"I can take a late lunch and see him then."

I could hardly believe it. This had to be from God. How or why my résumé kept showing up on this man's desk, I didn't know, but I was very excited. All my calls were in town that day, near The Henry Group's factory, so that afternoon I headed down Highway 34 to interview for a new job.

From the moment I walked into Ben Draper's office, I felt this was a God-ordained meeting. On the wall behind his desk hung a small plaque with the words *Stand Firm* in bold letters. Just below those words was the Scripture verse "Blessed is the man who perseveres under trial, because when he has stood the test, he will receive the crown of life that God has promised to those who love him" (James 1:12, NIV).

"I love that plaque," I said.

Ben smiled. "So do I," he said. "I told your wife that your résumé keeps turning up on my desk. Normally we throw them out after two years, but for some reason we kept this one. I figured that God must want me to talk to you."

Meeting with Ben felt more like a visit with an old friend than a job interview. As we talked, Ben and I discovered that we had a lot in common. He was a Christian and had decided a year ago to enter the ministry. I told him that I'd been heading in that direction for a while myself and that, in fact, my church was going to ordain me in April.

When the interview was over, Ben told me that I could have the job if I wanted it.

I was delighted, but I also knew this was something that Penny and I needed to discuss. "Let me go home and talk to my wife. We'll pray about it and get back to you," I told him.

It was pushing four o'clock when I headed back to the office. My day was almost finished, and I was looking forward to getting home.

LATE CALL

Back at the Praxair office in downtown Greenville, I began to make preparations to close out my day. I was going to be on call that weekend, so I needed to make sure my van was stocked with everything I might need. I had already delivered and set up a hospital bed, done several oxygen setups, and had a death call. All of that added to the excitement of the job interview had made for an exhausting day. As five o'clock drew near, I was ready for some quiet time and rest with my family.

I was just about to leave when the call came in. Somebody in Dallas needed an oxygen setup. I groaned. That would mean at least another four hours of work. I wasn't happy about it, but I was on call and had no choice.

As I pulled out of the parking lot, I called Penny to break the news. Matthew answered.

"Hey, Matthew, how you doin'?"

"Okay."

"Let me talk to Mama," I said.

When Penny came on the line, I said, "I just got a call for an oxygen setup in Dallas. Looks like it's going to be a late night and a long weekend."

Penny was sympathetic, as always. "I'm sorry. Do you have any idea of how long you'll be? Tommy's over here. He and Helen would like to take us all out for dinner."

I smiled. Tommy and Helen Gaston were our next-door neighbors and our dearest friends. In fact, Tommy and Helen were more than friends to us. They were practically parents. We had known them for years, ever since Penny began singing and playing piano in Tommy's southern gospel group. We weren't literally part of The Gaston family, but we might as well have been. I even had taken to calling Helen "Mama" because she was like a mother to me. One of the reasons we had bought that particular property in Alba was that we'd be living next door to Tommy and Helen. They loved to do things for us, and an invitation to take the whole family out to eat was not unusual. I hated to say no, but I was going to be back way too late to go out to dinner.

"I'm sorry, honey," I said. "I don't think I'll be back until nine or ten. Ask him if we can take a rain check."

The sun was setting in the western sky as I wheeled the van southward on Highway 34, toward Terrell. I needed to stop by our office there to pick up more oxygen concentrators. I was glad to be able to call Penny on my cell phone as I drove. I wasn't happy about having to work late that night, but at least I could have some company.

"So, how's Erin doing?" I asked.

"She seems fine," replied Penny.

"Have you heard anything from Charlie?"

"No, all's quiet. Why? Do you think he'll do something?"

"Probably not," I said. At first I had thought he might try some pranks or other kinds of harassment, but it looked as if that wasn't going to be a problem.

"What are the boys doing?" I asked.

"Watching TV."

We talked for quite a while, reflecting on the events of the past few days. It was good to have all the turmoil of Charlie behind us. Things would be better now, we agreed. And Erin would be happier, too.

I arrived at Praxair's Terrell office a little before six. I knew it was going to be a while before I ate supper, so I grabbed a Dr. Pepper and a banana-nut muffin from the refrigerator and then loaded the oxygen concentrators into my van.

As I had expected, it was after nine o'clock when finally I drove south on Highway 69 toward Alba. My mind raced as I thought of recent events. In just a little over a week I had lost my dad, cleaned out his apartment, held an estate sale, planned a funeral, made my daughter break up with her boyfriend, and received an offer out of the blue for a new job. It had been a rough couple of weeks, but all things considered, I felt that things were looking up.

Our future definitely appeared bright.

THE LAST GOOD TIME

I pulled the van into our driveway around nine thirty and breathed a deep sigh of relief. It had been a fourteen-hour workday, but at last I was home. Penny came out to meet me, as she had every time I had come home from work for the previous nineteen years. We kissed and went inside. The kids were watching a movie, and Penny went to warm up my dinner.

As I sat at the table eating spaghetti and garlic toast, Penny and I talked about the events of the day. We didn't discuss my new job opportunity, though. We didn't want to talk about it in front of the children until there was something definite to tell them.

After a few minutes, Penny asked if I'd mind if she got ready for bed. It had been a busy day for her, too, and she was tired. She wanted to get in bed and read for a while.

"No," I said. "Go ahead. I won't be far behind. I'm worn out."

Penny kissed the boys good night, but when she got to Erin, she asked, "Are you sure you gave back all of Charlie's things?"

Erin nodded. "Yes."

Penny pulled a pair of dog tags from her pocket and handed them to Erin. "Then why did I find Charlie's dog tags in your room?" she asked.

Erin flushed and grinned sheepishly.

"See to it that you give them back," said Penny as she kissed Erin good night.

I tried to finish my supper, but Penny had served me way too much food. On top of that, I was exhausted. Since my on-call weekends were usually quite full, I expected a busy Saturday. I decided to scrape what was left on my plate into the trash and head to bed. What followed was one of those parent-child moments that I might have quickly forgotten but now remains etched in my memory.

I don't know how I managed it, but when I went to scrape my plate, I spilled the spaghetti all over the floor. To make matters worse, when I tried to clean it up, I slipped on the mess and came crashing down in a heap on top of the plastic trash can.

That's when I heard the laughter.

Led by Matthew, all three kids were doubled over, whooping and laughing hysterically at the spectacle of their father sprawled in a pile of spaghetti sauce and trash.

"You think that's funny?" I asked, laughing.

I clambered to my feet, grabbed a pillow from the sofa, and hurled it at Matthew. He and Tyler quickly returned fire with pillows of their own, and soon we were in a full-blown pillow fight. But it didn't end there.

When I ran out of ammunition, I tackled Matthew and began to wrestle with him. Tyler jumped on top of me and tried to help his brother. Soon Erin joined in as we rolled around on the floor, laughing and squealing.

Eventually we all ran out of energy, and the party wound down.

I finished cleaning up the floor, then went and kissed each of the kids in turn.

"I love you," I said to each one.

As I turned to go to the bedroom, Matthew asked, "Can we stay up and finish watching the movie?"

"Okay," I said, "but keep the noise down. I've got an early day tomorrow. And don't stay up too late."

"We won't," they said.

I climbed into bed beside Penny. It was a good feeling, and I was more than ready to go to sleep. But Penny wanted to talk. She had questions about the job opportunity.

"So do you think you'll get the job?"

"He said it was mine if I wanted it," I replied.

"Do you?" she asked.

I nodded. "Uh-huh."

"Is the salary better?"

"Definitely."

"So what would you be doing?" she pressed.

I looked over at her. "Sweetheart, I'm really tired. Do you mind if we talk about it tomorrow? I promise, I'll tell you everything you want to know tomorrow."

Penny smiled her sweet smile. "Okay, Daddy. Good night."

"I love you," I said.

"I love you, too."

I leaned over and kissed her, then turned over and went to sleep.

* * *

The sound of a dog barking broke into my dreams. I blinked my eyes open and squinted at the digital clock beside my bed. It was 12:30 a.m.

Not now, Max, I thought.

Max, our black Lab, took his job seriously when it came to running off critters. As far out in the country as we lived, it wasn't unusual for coyotes or even wild pigs to roam through our property. And Max was always on the job—especially at night. I appreciated his heart, but tonight his timing was terrible. The last thing I needed was to have a good night's sleep disturbed. Some nights, I might have tried to quiet him, but I was too tired to bother.

"Oh, Max," I mumbled, "be quiet."

Max's barking faded away as I drifted back into a deep sleep.

CHAPTER 4

NIGHT TERRORS

When you pass through the waters, I will be with you;
And through the rivers, they will not overflow you.
When you walk through the fire, you will not be scorched,
Nor will the flame burn you. —ISAIAH 43:2

SOMETIME IN THE EARLY morning hours of Saturday, March 1, I awoke to the clang of our bedroom doorknob hitting the clothes dryer in the laundry room, just outside our bedroom. I thought maybe Tyler had had a bad dream and come downstairs to our bedroom. But before I could react, a series of deafening explosions filled the room.

I heard Penny's screams and opened my eyes.

A man stood in our bedroom doorway, silhouetted by the kitchen night-light. He had a gun in his hand. Disoriented and confused, I thought it was a robbery.

More gunfire erupted.

Penny moaned. I sat up and threw out my right arm to protect her. A flash and another explosion followed, and instantly my wrist felt as if someone had hit it with a sledgehammer. Another explosion hammered my forearm. Searing pain tore through my upper arm, then my shoulder. A final shot slammed into my right cheek and blew me out of the bed. I landed facedown, wedged into the narrow space between the bed and the wall.

Then the gunfire stopped.

I lay still as I heard the man walk over to my side of the bed. He kicked my feet, apparently checking to see if I was still alive. I closed my eyes tight and tried not to move. Then I heard metallic clicks. He was reloading.

In that instant, an amazing feeling of peace swept over me. I knew that when the killer finished reloading, he would shoot me in the back of the head and finish me off. I had no fear of dying. I knew that within a few seconds, I would be in God's presence.

I waited for the fatal shot. *Lord, please take me quickly.*

I relaxed and lost consciousness.

NO, CHARLIE! NO!

I must have been out only a few minutes.

When I awoke, the taste of blood and gunpowder filled my mouth. I tried to feel where I was wounded, but there wasn't enough room for me to move. I couldn't feel my right side, and my right arm wouldn't move.

Suddenly, the peace I'd felt moments ago vanished. *I'm going to die right here,* I thought. *If he comes back in and sees me breathing, he'll finish me off.*

I heard boots clomping on our hardwood floors—a sound that haunts me to this day. The intruder stomped back and forth in our living room, only a few feet away. I heard the crash of furniture being overturned and our possessions being smashed. A cacophony of notes came from Penny's piano as if someone had slammed both fists down on the keys. Whoever was out there must have swept Penny's knick-knacks off the top of the piano and onto the keys.

Who is it? Why is he doing this?

Amid the sounds of crashing furniture I could hear muffled voices, and for the first time I realized that there was more than one intruder. I couldn't understand what they were saying, but it was clear that there were at least two men in our house.

Then I heard shouting.

Matthew and Tyler were screaming and crying.

More shouts, then heavy footsteps started up the stairs, and I instantly panicked. The intruders weren't just after Penny and me; they were going to hurt the children, too.

I couldn't feel or move my right arm, so I tried to push myself up with my left. But my hand kept sliding in a thick pool of my own blood. Desperate to save my kids, I reached up and grabbed the bedsheets, trying to pull myself onto the mattress. At that instant I heard Matthew's hysterical pleas.

"Charlie, why are you doing this? No, Charlie! No!"

Gunfire rang out again and silenced Matthew.

At that instant I knew the identity of the intruder and why he was here. I realized that it was Charlie Wilkinson I had seen standing in our bedroom doorway and shooting at Penny and me.

I collapsed and passed out again. My last thought was that we were all going to die.

FIRE!

I woke up coughing; then I felt the heat.

I tried to look around, but I was blinded by smoke and the blood that had begun running into my eyes. I realized that Charlie and his companion had set the house on fire, but I was focused on trying to get up and help my family.

I managed to push myself up onto the bed. I looked across the room and saw Penny highlighted by the red-orange glow of the flames. She lay slumped against the wall. One look, and I knew she was gone. There was no chance to save her. My next thought was of Erin and the boys.

Two doors led out of our bedroom. One opened into the laundry room, which led to the bathroom and then the kitchen. The other—at the foot of our bed—gave access to the living room and the staircase up to the children's bedrooms. I had to get to Erin and the boys. I tried to go through that door and get to the stairs, but a wall of flames pushed me back into the bedroom.

Seconds later, flames covered the inside wall of our bedroom and stood between the only other door and me. I had to retreat to my side of the bed and climb over the bed to get to the other door. Maybe I could go through the kitchen to check on the kids.

On the other side of the bed I stopped one last time to check on Penny. I'd lost a lot of blood, but it was nothing compared to her. I had never seen so much blood in my life, and I will never forget that sight. I would never have left her if there had been any chance of saving her, but there wasn't. Penny was gone.

Nevertheless, I wanted to try to bring her with me, and I suppose I would have, but I had been shot at least five times, and my right arm was useless. I couldn't even drag Penny's body out of the burning house.

I moved toward the laundry-room door, struggling against blinding smoke and scorching heat. I felt as if I were inside an oven.

On the other side of the laundry room I tried to turn left into the kitchen, but the flames drove me back into the little hallway. I knew then that I couldn't get to the kids from inside the house.

My only option was to try to find my way to the bathroom window.

I felt as if I were drowning—drowning in smoke. I couldn't catch my breath. I tried to cover my nose and mouth with my one good arm.

It was a straight shot through our narrow bathroom to the window. If I could make it that far, I might be able to escape. When I got through the bathroom door, flames flowed up the wall on my left and curled over the ceiling, creating a tunnel of fire. Choking and blind, I felt my way forward through the blistering heat. My pajama pants and T-shirt felt red hot. If I didn't get out soon, I was sure they would catch fire.

I knew that the sink, toilet, and tub would all be on my right side, so I used my good arm to feel my way past the sink, past the toilet. But when I reached the shower curtain, I pushed too hard, lost my balance, and fell into the tub. Scrambling around in the bathtub, I panicked and lost track of where I was.

Stay calm. If you panic, you're dead.

I relaxed and got to my feet as quickly as I could manage. I covered my face with my good arm and felt for the bathtub's wall. When I found it, I followed it to my left and found the back corner. I knew the window was just to the left. I stood in the tub and felt along the wall until my fingers touched the window frame.

I carefully stepped out of the tub and tried to push the window open.

It wouldn't budge.

I pounded on it, hoping to break the glass, but I couldn't break it.

I knew I only had seconds left.

Come on. Come on!

I tried to unlock it, and as I fumbled with the latch, the window flew open. I punched the screen out of the window frame and stuck my head outside. For a few seconds, all I did was breathe the cool night air. I was like a drowning man whose head had just broken the surface of the water. I stayed where I was, gasping and clearing my lungs, but I knew I had to get the rest of the way out.

Fortunately the window was low enough that I didn't have to pull myself up. I squeezed my left arm and upper body through the frame and leaned out. Gravity took care of the rest. I toppled out of the window. It was about a five-foot drop to the ground outside the house, and the hard landing knocked the wind out of me. Oddly, I didn't feel much pain, but blood still filled my eyes, making it difficult to see.

Even though I was terrified and disoriented, I could think clearly enough to know that the killers might still be out there somewhere. I needed to find a hiding place quickly, where I could rest and collect myself.

I moved toward the side of the house and took cover behind our large propane tank.

CHAPTER 5

DARKNESS

You light my lamp;
The LORD my God illumines my darkness.
—PSALM 18:28

I'VE GOT TO HELP *the kids!*

I knew Penny was gone, but maybe there was still a chance of saving Tyler, Matthew, and Erin. I tried to make my way around to the front of the house, but as soon as I got there, I knew I couldn't get to them. Flames roared out of the front windows and blocked the only access I could have had.

Suddenly I realized that I was out in the open. I didn't know if Charlie and the other killer were still hanging around, so I retreated to the security of the propane tank and tried to collect my thoughts.

Only minutes ago, I had lain snuggled up to my wife, fast asleep.

Now, dazed and confused—almost in a trance—I cowered behind a full propane tank, only ten feet from a raging inferno.

I just need to wait, I thought. *Someone will call the police. Help is coming. I just need to hold on.*

As I crouched behind the tank, beads of sweat began to form on my brow. Between the heat of the burning house and the hot metal tank nearby, I felt as if I were sitting next to a furnace. Then reality crashed in: *This thing could blow!*

I had to find a safe place to wait for the authorities to arrive. So I turned and crawled on my belly toward the woods, just beyond a barbed-wire fence about fifty feet behind the house.

I crept under the fence and felt a sharp sting on my back as it snagged on the barbed wire. I ignored the pain and kept crawling until I reached a log about fifteen feet farther on. By that time, I was exhausted and needed rest. I crawled over the log and then lay down across it, facing the house. Now all I could do was wait.

Help will be here soon.

I waited and waited, but no one came.

I couldn't believe it. My house was almost fully engulfed in flames, and the noise was earsplitting at times. Windows exploded, sending out showers of glass. Other small explosions penetrated the roar caused by the uprush of flames. Part of the structure collapsed with a long, loud crack, just like the sound of a tree falling.

Surely somebody had heard that. Why hadn't they called 911? Why weren't the firefighters coming? After waiting a few more minutes, I realized that nobody was coming. If anybody was going to get help, it had to be me.

Tommy and Helen were our closest neighbors, but their house was almost four hundred yards away. To get there, I'd have to navigate blindly through a maze of woods thick with cedars and tall, long-needle pines, not to mention fallen branches, overgrown weeds, thorns, and just about any other natural obstacle you could imagine.

GOING FOR HELP

I didn't think about any of that. My only thought was that I needed to get help. On one level, I understood that my family was beyond help, but somehow I pushed those thoughts away. I felt that if I could just find someone to help us, everything would be all right.

And so I began the four-hundred-yard trek toward Tommy and Helen's. I learned later that it took me about an hour to cover a distance approximately the length of four football fields.

I stumbled forward until my legs gave out. I rested a few minutes, then pushed myself up and crawled. This was actually more difficult than walking, because my right arm hung useless and my left arm had to bear the entire load. I pulled myself forward with my good arm and pushed with my legs. Thorns clawed at me, but I didn't notice the pain. I was running on pure adrenaline.

Every now and then I stopped and looked back to where my house was rapidly being overtaken by the flames.

Shock, confusion, denial, despair, and hope all swirled in my head, but nothing made sense. Everything felt surreal, almost like a dream sequence in a movie. I felt as if I were walking in a fog. The only thing that made sense was finding help. I felt that if I could just get to Tommy and Helen's, they would fix everything.

The trauma had not only sent me into a mental fog; it had also dulled my other senses. Although it was only about forty degrees outside and I was wearing only a T-shirt and pajama pants, I didn't feel the cold. I had been shot in the face, torso, back, and arm, and I knew I'd lost a lot of blood, yet I felt no pain to speak of. The only senses that still seemed to be working fine were my senses of smell and taste. I still tasted blood and gunpowder, and nothing I did would make it go away. The smell of the smoke stayed with me too.

After resting a few minutes, I would push myself back to my feet and walk forward until my legs gave out again. I'd rest awhile, then crawl until I couldn't make it any farther. I'd rest some more and start the process all over again. Every cycle of walking and crawling became more difficult. I wasn't even sure I'd make it all the way, but I knew I had to try.

I went on this way for a long time, and the farther I went into the thick woods, the darker it got. It wasn't long until I couldn't see my hand in front of my face. I'd look behind me now and then, and I could still see the glow from my burning house. It was bright against the night sky, but not strong enough to light my way through the thick trees and brush.

Staggering like a drunken blind man, I struggled on, occasionally tripping over fallen branches and coming up with a mouthful of dirt. More than once I walked straight into the trunk of a tall pine tree. Every bump, every fall, every inch I crawled sapped precious energy and made it harder to press on.

I was about halfway to Tommy and Helen's house when I felt as if I were going to pass out. I had to sit down and rest. I leaned up against the trunks of two intertwined trees and slid to the ground. Every breath brought a stab of pain, and I wondered if one of my lungs had collapsed.

As I sat there gasping for breath, I turned my attention to my house. Even through the thick woods, I could still see the glow of the fire. As I watched the sparks and smoke soaring over the trees toward heaven, a wave of despair washed over me. My throat thickened, and tears filled my eyes, blurring what little vision I had.

They're gone.

I finally understood that trying to get help was pointless. Penny, Erin, Matthew, and Tyler were dead, and no effort on my part would bring them back. I sobbed.

What am I going to do without them? Oh, God, what am I going to do?

I didn't understand any of what was happening, but most of all I couldn't understand why God had turned His back on us and allowed this. I wanted it to be over.

"Lord, just take me now," I said. "I can't go on."

I sat and watched the flames, waiting for the Lord to take me home to be with my family.

Then, out of the blue, came a thought: *If I die, nobody will know who did this.*

I looked toward Tommy and Helen's house, and for the first time I saw a flickering light coming from their property. It was faint, but it was there. At first I thought it might be a flashlight, and for a few seconds hope filled my heart.

Tommy's coming.

But the light didn't move, and I soon realized that whatever it was, it wasn't Tommy.

As I sat watching that light, I knew it was decision time. If I stayed where I was, someone would find me dead in the morning. But if I pressed on toward that light, I could do one final thing for my family.

I didn't care if I died; in fact, I wanted to. I had no desire to go on living without Penny and the kids. But before I could join them, I had one last job to do. I hadn't been able to save my family, but I could do something to bring closure to this horrible event. I was going to make sure that someone knew it was Charlie Wilkinson who had done this.

I pulled myself to my feet and started walking.

PUSH TO THE FINISH LINE

I pushed forward with a resolve that I can't explain or even understand. I only had to make it to Tommy and Helen's. No farther. Once I identified the killers, I could drift away and join Penny and the kids, but that was not going to happen until my work was done.

I resumed my pattern: Walk four or five steps. Sit down and rest.

Crawl a few feet. Sit and rest. Then do it all over again. Always, always keeping my eyes fixed on the light.

After a brief rest, I had just started walking again when the ground vanished beneath my feet. I lurched and fell face first into ice-cold water. For a few seconds the cold water took my breath away, leaving me sputtering and gasping for breath. I tried to grab something, anything, but all I got was a handful of mud. Finally, my mind cleared enough for me to understand what had happened.

I had fallen into the creek that crossed our land about two-thirds of the way to Tommy's property. At the moment, it held only about a foot of water, but the drop was nearly four feet. After a big rain, that creek could quickly become a rushing torrent. If it had been full and flowing that night, I probably would have drowned. As it was, that cold water did me a favor. It shocked my system and gave it a wake-up call. Even so, I had to climb a four-foot embankment to get out of the creek. No easy task with only one functioning arm. If I hadn't already made up my mind to identify the murderers, I might have given up and died right there.

In the pitch-blackness, I felt around on the side of the bank. I found some tree roots sticking out a few feet to my right. I grabbed hold of the roots and used them to pull myself up. Then I dug my fingers into the ground beyond the creek and clawed my way out. When my torso was out of the creek bed, I fell forward and lay there, my legs still hanging down into the creek.

After a minute or two, I began to pull again with my good arm. I dug into the dirt and grass and slowly inched the rest of my body out. When I was finally on dry ground, I lay there, gasping and trying to catch my breath. I don't know how long I stayed there, but eventually I got to my feet and started to walk again. But I must have stood up too quickly, because my head swam and I collapsed. I lay there awhile longer, then got to my feet again, a little slower this time.

From the time I crawled out of the creek, I never looked back at my house again. I knew that if I did, I'd lose hope and give up. Looking ahead, I still couldn't see anything. There was no moonlight. All I could see was the flickering light coming from Tommy and Helen's, and I knew that was my goal.

I continued to stumble and crawl forward, but confused and disoriented as I was, I didn't realize that I was moving in a diagonal line toward the road and away from Tommy and Helen's house. When I hit another barbed-wire fence, panic surged through me. I was so close, but the farther I went, the more difficult each obstacle became. I didn't know if I could manage to climb this fence.

I could see the faint outline of Tommy and Helen's house now. The light was coming from their front window—a night-light or something. I was almost at the finish line. I couldn't give up, not when I was this close. Desperately weak, I somehow managed to climb through the barbed wire and almost immediately ran into another barrier.

Tommy and Helen's front gate stood open and pushed back against the barbed-wire fence I'd just climbed through. The gate wasn't latched, and I could easily have pushed it forward and gotten past it, but my mind wasn't working. All I knew was that here was another fence to get past. I felt along the gate and stumbled toward the right. Eventually I found the metal-pipe fence to which the gate was attached. I leaned over and climbed through the pipes, finally feeling concrete under my bare feet.

Tommy and Helen's driveway followed a gentle upward slope with a curve to the right. Under normal circumstances, it is an easy walk. But at that moment, it might as well have been Mount Everest. That last little stretch would be the hardest of my entire journey.

Then I felt as if I had a drill sergeant shouting in my ear: "Go on! Keep going! You can do this! Don't quit! You can make it!"

With one last burst of determination, I fastened my eyes on the front door, leaned forward, and staggered up the driveway. Every step was torture, but every step also brought Tommy and Helen's house more clearly into view.

My legs felt like lead, but I would not stop. Somehow I knew that if I sat down, I'd never get up again.

It took the last ounce of strength I had left to make it the length of that driveway. And when I reached the Gastons' front door, I collapsed. I couldn't have stood up again if I'd tried.

But my job wasn't finished yet. It was the middle of the night, and Tommy and Helen were asleep. I had to wake them up and tell them what happened.

I lay on my side and lifted my good arm. I didn't have the strength to make a fist and knock; it was all I could do to lift my arm. I flopped my elbow and forearm against the door, hoping the sound would be loud enough. I don't know how many times I had to throw my arm against the door, but I thought Tommy would never come.

Finally the porch light came on, and he opened the door.

"Oh, my God. Helen, come quick!"

Tommy came out and bent down to talk to me. "What happened?"

"We need help," I said. "Charlie came and shot us all."

"What about Penny and the kids?" he asked.

A tidal wave of grief swept over me.

"They're all dead."

CHAPTER 6

911

My strength is dried up like a potsherd,
And my tongue cleaves to my jaws;
And You lay me in the dust of death.

—PSALM 22:15

"DON'T LEAVE ME, MAMA. I think I'm going to die. Please don't leave me."

Helen Gaston's soft, reassuring voice broke through my hysteria. "Don't worry, Terry. I won't leave you."

Tommy tried to help me to my feet, but I had no strength left. I couldn't move.

"Helen, help me get him inside."

They got underneath each arm, lifted me up, and dragged me into the house.

Maybe it was the warmth of the house. Maybe it was because I was safe now. Whatever the reason, as soon as I was inside, the pain kicked in. Up till then, I'd felt very little pain, but now it was almost as if someone had turned on a switch in my brain. All at once I felt sharp, burning pain all through my body. And I felt cold.

Seconds later, I heard Tommy talking to the 911 operator. His voice was calm and controlled. I listened, wondering how long it would take for help to get there.

"This is Tommy Gaston. I've got a man that's been shot. He's out here at my house now. . . . Okay."

A few seconds passed. Then he started all over. "This is Tommy Gaston. I've got a man that's been shot out here at my house. . . . Yes." Tommy tried to give the operator his address but stumbled at the county-road number. Helen helped him.

"Right. Well, yes, it's Rains County. That's Alba, actually."

Then it sounded almost like Tommy lost the connection.

"Hello?" A few seconds' pause. "Hello! . . . Yes. . . . I'm sorry I can't—yes!"

Tommy was beginning to sound frustrated.

"I don't know. Just a little bit ago. And we've also got a house on fire out here. . . Yes, he's right here with me. I don't know any more details. I've got to hang up and help him."

The longer Tommy stayed on the line, the more frustrated he sounded.

"Yes, he's bleeding. . . . Yes, he's awake. . . . I don't know. I don't know, but I've got to go. Just get somebody out here. . . . I don't know! He's bloody all over. . . . No! I don't know."

I lay there bleeding, and Tommy wanted desperately to help me. Finally, he gave up on the 911 call and hung up the phone. "Get him a towel, Helen—Helen, get him a towel."

They brought me towels and tried to stop the bleeding, but there were just too many wounds.

A few minutes later, my former pastor, Brother Wayne Wolfe, and his wife arrived. Tommy had called him right after he called 911. I was disoriented and in pain. I don't remember much, other than that they all looked and sounded very worried.

"Hang in there, Terry," they told me. "Help is on the way."

Minutes later I found myself surrounded by EMTs and sheriff's deputies, all asking me questions at the same time.

"Mr. Caffey, can you hear me?"

"Who did this?"

"Where does it hurt?"

"Did you see your assailant?"

"Can you feel this?"

Pain surged through me when the paramedics lifted me onto the gurney. I screamed.

The EMTs wheeled me out of the house and toward the ambulance. Every bump and jostle shot a fresh wave of pain through me. When I was in the back of the ambulance, Detective Almon from the Rains County Sheriff's Department introduced himself to me.

"I think I'm going to die," I told him.

"Who did this?" he asked.

"Charlie Wilkinson."

I struggled to concentrate through the haze of pain that clouded my mind.

"I woke up and saw somebody standing in my bedroom with a gun. I think it was a shotgun. When I put my arm up to shield us, he shot me. After that, I blacked out. When I woke up, I heard my oldest son, Matthew, yelling out, 'Charlie!' Charlie Wilkinson is my daughter's ex-boyfriend. Then I heard more gunshots. I passed out after that.

"When I woke up again, there was fire everywhere. I tried to get upstairs to save the children, but I couldn't get to them. After that I got out of the house through the bathroom window and went over to Tommy and Helen Gaston's."

"Are you sure it was Charlie? Did you see him, or are you just speculating?"

"I saw him," I said. "And I heard Matthew shout his name."

I heard another voice say, "I know Charlie."

Seconds later, the ambulance door closed, and we were on our way.

EMERGENCY ROOMS

The ambulance tore down our rough county road, siren blaring. The ride was bumpy, the pain excruciating. I groaned.

The paramedic tried to reassure me. "Hang in there," he said. "We'll be there soon."

I looked at the ceiling and tried to find something to focus on, some way of distracting myself. I wanted to let go and cry, but I couldn't. Not in front of this stranger. Finally, I decided to focus my attention on the siren. It was the only way I could maintain control. I'd never felt so alone in my life.

They're all gone. I've got no one to help me get through this. No one.

I don't know how long it took us to get there, but once the ambulance arrived at the Hopkins County Memorial Hospital in Sulphur Springs, the relative quiet of the ambulance ride exploded into chaos.

They bumped and jostled me again as they pulled the gurney from the ambulance and pushed me into the emergency room. More pain.

The ER felt like a refrigerator. Again people surrounded me, all talking at once.

"Why'd you bring him here?" I heard a doctor say to one of the EMTs. "We're not a trauma center."

"This was the closest place," he responded. "We didn't know where else to take him."

They wanted to CareFlight me to Dallas but couldn't because it was too foggy.

"He needs to be at a trauma center," the doctor repeated. "We'll stabilize him and send him on."

"Mr. Caffey, can you hear me?"

I nodded.

"We need to get you to a trauma center where they can take care of you. Do you want to go to Dallas or Tyler?"

I don't remember whether I said, "Tyler" or "I don't care." They sent me to Tyler.

Once the medical team in Sulphur Springs had finished patching me up, I felt myself being wheeled out to the ambulance again, this time for the trip to Tyler. An officer rode with me in the ambulance and questioned me some more.

When we arrived at the East Texas Medical Center in Tyler, the chaos started all over again. Doctors and nurses moving around and talking to one another. I couldn't make out most of what they were saying. Then came another round of the same questions I had already answered.

As the doctors and nurses were talking to one another and working on me, I heard another voice.

"Mr. Caffey, I'm a detective with the Tyler Police Department. We're going to do some swabs on your hands and take some swabs from the inside of your jaw. Do you have any problem with that? Is that okay? Do you agree to that?"

It was all I could do to talk. My sinus cavities were full of blood, and I couldn't breathe through my nose. I said, "Yes," but my voice was barely a whisper.

"Can you tell me if you've been around a gun tonight?"

"No."

"You haven't been around a gun. Have you handled a gun?"

"No."

"You haven't handled one either?"

I shook my head.

"But you were shot, correct?"

I nodded, "Uh-huh."

"And you haven't handled a gun at all in the last twenty-four hours or so?"

"No."

"We'd like to take some scrapings under your fingernails. Is that okay?"

"Yes, that's okay."

"I know you've relived this several times, but can you tell me so I'll know what happened?"

I went through the whole story again but wondered why I had to keep repeating it. *My family is dead. Why do they keep asking me all these questions? Am I a suspect?*

I wondered why they weren't out looking for the ones who killed my family. I was angry, confused, grief-stricken, and in incredible pain. All I knew was that I wanted the questions to stop.

In the relative calm after the officers had left, I noticed the awful taste of blood and gunpowder. I wanted so badly to get it out of my mouth, but they'd told me that I couldn't have any water.

Eventually, a doctor came to explain the nature of my injuries and what the medical team was going to do. To my surprise, the news was good, at least as far as my injuries were concerned. According to the doctor, several of my wounds were "clean through" shots, with clear entry and exit wounds. Charlie or his accomplice had shot me at least twice in the back. None of the bullets—not even the one that struck me in the face—hit any major organs or blood vessels. A few came very close, and if any of those had been even a fraction of an inch different in one direction or another, I probably would never have gotten off the bedroom floor. One bullet lodged in my shoulder and another in my rotator cuff. They would have to take those out surgically.

The shot that hit my upper right arm had damaged a nerve. That explained the numbness on my right side and my useless right arm.

The doctor said that they were going to go in and repair it. I would probably regain the use of my arm, but he couldn't be sure whether it would be total or partial.

The bullet that hit the right side of my face traveled at an angle through my sinus cavities, broke both cheekbones, and amazingly, exited through my left ear canal. They would do surgery on Sunday to repair that damage. For at least four weeks after the shootings, I wasn't allowed to blow my nose. And for some time when I'd clean my left ear, the cotton swab would come out dark with gunpowder residue. But even with such a severe injury, my hearing was undamaged.

Looking back, I can see God's hand in preserving my life, but that's not how I felt about it then. All I knew was that I was alone. My wife and children were dead. Everything I owned had been destroyed. And now the doctor had told me that I was going to survive.

Most people would have considered that good news.

I did not.

I couldn't face life by myself.

"Mr. Caffey," a nurse said, "we're going to give you some morphine to help you with the pain."

I nodded.

They injected the morphine into my IV tube. Seconds later, my pain dissolved, and everything went black.

CHAPTER 7

CRITICAL

He has filled me with bitterness,
He has made me drunk with wormwood.
He has broken my teeth with gravel;
He has made me cower in the dust.
—LAMENTATIONS 3:15-16

DESPITE THE HORRORS of the night, Saturday dawned with a glimmer of hope.

Shortly before the Tyler police detective interviewed me the night before, my sister Mary had come over to my bed and said, "Terry, we've got good news."

Good news? How could there be any good news?

"Erin made it out of the house. She's alive."

Erin is alive?

Because the doctors had decided to wait until Sunday to do surgery, they kept me sedated the rest of Saturday. Much of the day was a fog, but as I slipped in and out of consciousness, I felt hopeful for the first time since all of this had started. Somehow my daughter had escaped that burning house. Maybe I still had something to live for.

In one of my more lucid moments I asked Mary, "What happened? How did Erin get out?"

"They're saying she escaped from a second-story window and then ran and hid in the woods."

"Where is she?"

"They took her to the hospital in Sulphur Springs to get her checked out," said Mary. "As soon as she's done, they'll bring her down here to see you."

I nodded, grateful for the news. I can't even describe how good it felt to know that Erin had survived.

But as I lay there, I began to puzzle over what Mary had told me.

How could Erin have escaped from a second-story window? She couldn't have escaped from her own room. I had installed an air conditioner in her window and had anchored it with screws. She would have needed a drill to get it out. Maybe she got out through the boys' window.

Another question began to nag. Mary had told me that Erin ran into the woods and hid. If so, why didn't she hear me out there? Why didn't she come and find me?

The questions bothered me, but the morphine kept me from spending much time or energy thinking about them. Besides, the important thing was that Erin had survived. I couldn't wait to see her. We'd get through this together.

I relaxed and drifted off to sleep.

SHATTERED

"Where's Erin?" I asked. "Is she here yet?"

"No," said Mary. "But she's on her way. She'll be here soon."

"Who's got her?"

"She's with her grandparents."

I nodded. That was good. Larry and Virginia Daily were Penny's parents. Erin had always been close to them. They'd be able to comfort each other.

It's difficult to maintain any sense of time when you're under heavy sedation, but I remember waiting and waiting, expecting Erin to come. Finally, after about an hour and a half, I asked Mary, "Where are they? Is something wrong?"

"Nothing's wrong," she said soothingly. "Try to relax."

I did try, but I wanted to see my daughter. I wanted to compare notes and see if she could shed some light on what had happened. Maybe she had seen something that I hadn't, knew something I didn't.

As time passed, I noticed that people were acting strange around me. They avoided me and wouldn't make eye contact. When well over two hours had passed since Mary had told me that Erin was on her way, I asked again.

"Mary, what's going on?"

I could see hesitancy in her expression. There was clearly something she didn't want to tell me.

"They told me not to tell you," she said, her voice softening. "They said it would get you upset. You're still critical, and they don't want anything to upset you." She paused and took my hand. "I can't go on seeing you like this. You have a right to know."

"Know what?"

Mary paused again.

"Just tell me, Mary. Just tell me. What's going on?"

Sadness etched her face as she said, "They've arrested Erin. They're saying she was involved."

In that instant my fragile hope shattered into a million pieces, and I exploded. "No way!" Grief, fury, frustration, confusion, and a host of other emotions boiled up, all at the same time, and I screamed, "There is *no way* she was involved in this. No way! No way! No way!"

For a few short hours, I had had my daughter back. Now I felt as if I had lost her again.

I felt hollow as I lay in the ICU, awaiting surgery to remove the bullets that were still inside me and to repair the damage to my face. In less than twenty-four hours I had lost everything. My house was gone, along with all its contents. That didn't mean much by itself. Things could be replaced. But I could never replace the children I'd lost—and I could never replace my Penny.

PENNY

Our marriage wasn't arranged, but our first meeting certainly was—although I didn't find out till later.

I was in my early twenties and had been living on my own for a couple of years when I dropped by my parents' house one afternoon after work.

"There's a revival service at Gatewood Baptist Church tonight," my mother said. "You ought to come with us."

I was a professing Christian, but I'd stopped attending church after I'd gotten out on my own. I shook my head. "Naw, I don't want to go to church tonight. Besides, I don't have anything to wear."

My mother wasn't so easily defeated. "Don't tell me you don't have anything to wear. You still have church clothes right back there in your closet."

I hemmed and hawed. I'd just finished a long day at work as a supervisor in a wood shop in Dallas. I really didn't want to go to church that night.

"No, I don't think so," I said.

Then my mother went in for the kill.

"Well," she said, "there's this cute blonde there who's been asking about you. And she's single."

I backpedaled quickly. "Whoa. Wait a minute. Who's this blonde? How does she know about me?"

I learned later that my parents' next-door neighbor was playing the role of matchmaker. She had already told my mother about Penny, and she'd mentioned to Penny that her next-door neighbors had an unmarried son who was living on his own. It was a setup from the beginning.

Even the pastor's wife was in on the plan.

Penny regularly drove several high school boys to church, and they usually sat with her during the service. The pastor's wife told the boys to sit somewhere else that night, because if I saw them sitting by Penny, I might think one of them was her boyfriend.

To be honest, I didn't expect much that night. After all, even though this was a church service, it was essentially equivalent to a blind date. If this girl needed to be fixed up with someone, how pretty could she be?

My questions evaporated the instant I saw Penny. She was cute and petite and had a beautiful smile. And she could play piano like nobody I'd ever heard before. Maybe it's a stretch to say that it was love at first sight, but Penny and I fell in love quickly. We went on our first date the next week. Eight months later we were married.

Penny was a servant. She avoided the spotlight and didn't even like to have her picture taken. But wherever she saw a need, she was there to help. Early in our marriage, our church needed a Vacation Bible School director. Penny didn't like being in charge, but no one else would take the job. Reluctantly, she agreed and did a fantastic job.

When VBS was over, the church wanted to give her a gift to recognize a job well done, but she wouldn't accept it. Instead, she asked that it go to one of the other workers.

Penny demonstrated her servant's heart right up to the end. When the children went back to public school after being home-schooled, she didn't feel comfortable just staying at home all day, so she volunteered with the local chapter of Meals on Wheels. It gave her something to do, but more important to her was that she was helping people.

Penny also played a part in the most important event of my life—my coming to faith in Christ. Although I was a professing believer when we got married, I didn't truly know Jesus Christ as my Savior. My relationship with Him was based strictly on head knowledge.

I grew up in a Bible-believing church, and one Sunday morning when I was about nine or ten, some of my friends responded to an invitation to come to Christ. Not wanting to be left out, I went along with them and told the man up front that I wanted to be baptized. I didn't talk to anyone, and if someone explained the gospel to me, I don't remember it. All I know is that a few weeks later we were all going to be baptized.

I lined up behind my friends, waiting my turn to go into the baptistry with the pastor. A deacon who stood beside me quietly whispered in my ear, "Now, does this baptism save you?"

"Yes," I answered.

He shook his head. "No, baptism is a public confession of your faith in Christ. It doesn't save you. You're saved by believing in Jesus."

I didn't understand what he meant, but there was no time for clarification. The next thing I knew, the pastor called my name, and up I went into the baptistry. When I came up out of the water, I thought I was saved.

I continued believing that I was a born-again Christian for years. I even worked in youth ministry and taught Sunday school, knowing all the right words but never internalizing them. After Penny and I married, I occasionally experienced periods of uncertainty about my faith. It worried Penny, and we discussed it several times.

"Are you sure you're a Christian?" Penny would ask.

I'd think about it for a while and then say, "Yeah, I'm saved. It's just Satan working on my mind."

Years later, when we were living in Celeste, Texas, God brought me to a crisis point. First Baptist Church of Celeste was holding a tent-revival week. Penny couldn't go one night because one of the kids was sick, so I went by myself. The message was just what I needed.

The evangelist described how he had thought he was saved at a very young age but in reality he hadn't known Christ at all. That hit me hard. I felt as if he were talking just to me.

I thought about what he said all the way home and through the next workday. The more I thought about it, the less sure of my salvation I became. As I drove home, I began to cry. I was convinced that I had never genuinely trusted in Jesus Christ. When I was baptized, I had simply been performing an outward act with no basis in an inward reality. God brought me under such deep conviction of my sin and my need for Christ that by the time I got home from work, I was sobbing uncontrollably.

Penny met me at the door but couldn't quite figure out what was wrong with me. I tried to tell her, but I couldn't make myself clear.

The children were watching TV, and she didn't want them to be worried, so she led me into the bedroom and then asked what was wrong.

"I'm lost," I told her. "I need Christ."

"What?" she asked.

I explained about the previous night's message. "I'm lost," I concluded. "I need to trust Christ as my Savior."

At that, Penny started looking around the bedroom.

"What are you looking for?" I asked.

"We need to read the Scriptures," she said, searching frantically for her Bible.

Finally I caught her and said, "Penny, you don't need to read me the Scriptures." I pointed to my head. "I've got all that up here. I just need to get down and pray. Will you pray with me?"

Penny and I knelt beside our bed, and I asked Jesus Christ to be my Savior.

Penny had been a servant, a wonderful wife and mother, and my best friend. And now she was gone.

VISITS

At my request, a deputy sheriff from Emory and a Texas Ranger came to see me on Monday, a day after my surgery. Much of what had happened the night of the murders was still a huge blank for me. My family and the hospital staff wouldn't tell me much or let me watch the news, so while I knew that Erin was accused of involvement in the crime, I didn't know how deeply.

"I guess the first thing I want to know is how my daughter is. Is she okay?"

"She is," the officer said. "She's doing fine. She's at the juvenile detention facility in Greenville."

"I don't want to know a lot of details," I said, "but what kind of involvement did she have?"

The officer paused. He seemed hesitant to tell me. Finally he said, "Her involvement is great."

I'd been holding myself together fairly well up to that point, but when he said that, I fell apart. "Why? Why? I don't understand."

I'd already learned that a twenty-year-old man named Charles Waid was the second shooter, and that a young woman named Bobbi Johnson had driven the getaway car. But the most difficult thing to accept was that Charlie, Charles, and Bobbi had all pointed the finger of blame at Erin. They said that she was responsible for everything and that the murders had been her idea.

The thought that my daughter was not only involved but may have masterminded the murders of her mother and brothers was more than I could bear. I had never felt so forsaken in my life.

But although I felt forsaken and alone, I really wasn't. More people were there for me than I could ever imagine. I didn't know it at the time, but nearly 150 people showed up at the emergency room. Family, fellow church members, my pastor and former pastors, coworkers, friends, and acquaintances all flocked to Tyler to be with me and offer support. In fact, there were so many people that it caused logistical problems for the hospital. Only a few were allowed in to see me, but the others still wanted to be there to encourage, comfort, and pray. Later, after surgery and once I was in my own room, a steady stream of visitors trickled in to see me.

Some visits were uncomfortable when people didn't know what to do or say. They wanted to show me that they cared, but what do you say to a man who has just had three family members murdered and has himself barely survived? What do you say to someone whose daughter has been arrested and charged as an accomplice in those crimes? How do you talk to someone who, on top of all these tragedies, has lost everything he owned?

Some people tried to lighten the mood by telling humorous stories. It felt as if they thought they could make the all the horror disappear with a joke. When this happened, it made me angry, although I never showed it. I couldn't understand why people were trying to be funny.

I've lost my family! I thought. *There's nothing funny about that. Why is everybody laughing?*

Of course, those people didn't mean to be unkind or insensitive. They meant well on their visits, and I appreciate that. The truth is, most of us really don't know how to act around people who are suffering.

We want to help, but we find silence uncomfortable. We feel the need to say something, but we don't want to lose control of our own emotions, believing that somehow that would make things worse for the one who's suffering. We don't want to shed our own tears in front of the person we've come to comfort. And so we try to lighten the atmosphere, distract the suffering person so that we don't have to face the horrible reality.

I understand that now, but it bothered me then.

There were some other visits that week that I will never forget. Visits like the one I received from my friend Brother Joe Pierce.

Brother Pierce is pastor of Daugherty Baptist Church in Emory. We weren't members there, but we loved to visit. We enjoyed Joe's preaching and dropped by occasionally to hear him. In fact, we had visited just a few weeks before the murders.

Brother Joe is Texan through and through, and he loves to dress Western style. On one of the Sundays when we visited, he wore a beautiful Western belt with a shiny chrome horseshoe buckle. After the service, I commented on his belt. "I really like that," I said. "Where'd you get it?"

"It was a gift," he replied.

I eyed him up and down and said, "Hmm. We're about the same size. I think that belt would look a whole lot better on me." We both laughed. I was kidding, and he knew it.

In the hospital, Brother Joe wept openly as he stood by my bed. In his hands he held a white plastic Wal-Mart bag. As we talked, my eyes kept drifting to the bag he was holding. I knew he had brought me something, but I couldn't figure out what it was.

Still weeping, he said, "Terry, I loved your family so much. I just don't know what to do. I can't afford to buy you nothin', but I want you to have this."

He handed me the Wal-Mart bag. I fumbled with my left hand, trying to get it open. Finally, my fingers touched leather, and I knew without looking what he'd brought me. Out of the bag came that Western belt.

Most people probably wouldn't think of giving someone a belt as a condolence gift, but it was just what I needed. Joe Pierce gave me something of himself.

A few days later my pastor, Todd McGahee from Miracle Faith Baptist Church, brought another gift, this time from Ben Draper of The Henry Group.

It seemed like an eternity since I had sat in Ben's office interviewing for a new job. In reality, it had been less than a week. Pastor Todd brought the plaque that I'd admired in Ben's office. Ben sent it through Todd along with a message. He said that whenever I was ready, he had a job waiting for me. He also told me that he had a trailer in Alba that I could use if I needed someplace to stay.

I held the plaque in my hands and read the verse: "Blessed is a man who perseveres under trial; for once he has been approved, he will receive the crown of life which the Lord has promised to those who love Him" (James 1:12). Only a few days earlier, that verse had resonated with me. Now when I read it, I just felt empty.

Many others came that week to pray, to encourage, to show me they cared. I don't remember most of the visits. The pain medication kept me in a perpetual fog. But I didn't mind that, because whenever the medication wore off and the fog cleared for a while, I found myself drowning in grief.

CHAPTER 8

RECOVERY

My soul has been rejected from peace;
I have forgotten happiness.
So I say, "My strength has perished,
And so has my hope from the LORD.*"*
—LAMENTATIONS 3:17-18

I DIDN'T WANT to think about life beyond my hospital room.

My hospital stay lasted only about six days—pretty remarkable, considering the fact that I had entered the hospital in critical condition from multiple gunshot wounds, including one to the face. I recovered quickly from the physical trauma, but my emotional struggles were just beginning.

The hospital became a refuge for me. My little room was a cocoon that shielded me from the awful reality of my new life. The hospital staff met all my needs. I had no worries about food or shelter, no pressures from a job. The nurses even managed my pain. When I began to hurt too much, I pushed a button, and soon morphine came to my rescue. My sole responsibility was to lie there, recover, and entertain the occasional visitor.

One day Roger Pippin, one of my coworkers from Praxair, came to see me. In his hands he held a Bible.

"I was on my way to see you and wondering what I could get you. I know people have been donating money and clothes, but I got to wondering if anybody had brought you a Bible," he said.

I shook my head.

"I had to pass by my church on the way down here," Roger continued. "I have a key, so I thought I'd look around and see if they had any extras lying around. I know you like the King James, so I brought you this," he said, handing me the Bible.

It wasn't anything fancy. Just the kind of Bible you could find at any Wal-Mart or Dollar Store. Black imitation-leather cover with gold leaf on the edges of the pages. The words *Holy Bible* in gold on the front.

I turned it over in my hands. The truth was, I had no desire to read it. In fact, I hadn't prayed since the attack on my house. Why should I? God had let me down.

I had committed myself and my family to serving Him. I had taught my children well and brought them up to follow Him. I had kept my family in church. I had done everything I knew to do. But then God allowed all this to happen.

God didn't just take my family; He took them in the most brutal of ways. He allowed the killers to burn my house down and destroy everything I owned. On top of that, He allowed my daughter to be arrested and charged with complicity in the murders. I felt as if God had forsaken me. Why would I want to read His word? Would it somehow make sense of all this? I didn't think so.

Of course, I didn't want to dump all that on Roger. He had come out of kindness and concern for me, and the gift he had brought was from the heart. So I thanked him when I set the Bible down on my bedside table.

"I appreciate that, Roger. Thanks."

"You know, maybe you ought to read the book of Job. You have a lot in common with him."

I nodded and smiled, but inwardly I bristled. I'd read the book of Job many times. And Job and I definitely had a lot in common. Both of us had lost our possessions, our families, and our health. But I didn't want suggestions for a Bible-reading program right then. I wanted to stay in a drug-induced fog and not have to think about everything that had happened.

After Roger left, my mind wandered. I thought of my dad's funeral the week before and about how Matthew and I had played a harmonica duet. I wondered if his harmonicas had survived the fire.

MATTHEW

We had called him Bubba as far back as I could remember, but Matthew desperately wanted us to stop. He was thirteen and thought his nickname sounded too childish. So when he went back to public school, he made sure all the teachers called him Matthew. At church it was more difficult. Most of the people there had been calling him Bubba most of his life. So they'd slip now and then and have to catch themselves and apologize.

"Sorry, Bubba—I mean—Matthew."

Even Penny and I occasionally forgot and called him Bubba in public. Matthew would roll his eyes and sigh. We'd apologize and promise to try harder, but it wasn't easy. In any case, he was always Bubba at home.

The nickname fit. Matthew was definitely a "bubba," a big,

soft-spoken, gentle bear of a boy. Although he had always been big, in the past year he had really shot up. But despite his football-player size, Matthew wouldn't hurt a fly. He had an amazingly tender heart.

When he was eight years old, we went to a Christmas program at a friend's church. Matthew wanted to have a better view, so he sat by himself, several pews ahead of us. During the service, the pastor explained that they were taking an offering for a family whose house had recently burned down.

Matthew had worked hard for months, saving money to buy Christmas presents for all of us. He'd saved up about forty dollars. As the offering plate came around, we saw him take out his wallet and put some money in. I turned to Penny and said, "It looks like he put in all of it."

After the service was over, I talked to him about it.

"Did you put all your money in the offering plate?"

He looked up at me and nodded. "Yes."

"You didn't have to put all your money in. Why did you do that?"

He shrugged. "I thought they needed it more than we did."

Even at eight, that's the kind of person he was.

Over the last few months of his life, Matthew had kept a journal as an assignment for school. It was the perfect thing for him. He was shy and didn't talk a lot, so his journal opened a window into his mind and heart.

Because Matthew kept the journal at school, it wasn't lost in the fire. His teacher gave the little notebook to our pastor, Todd McGahee, to pass on to me. As I read his entries, I saw again and again the kind of boy Matthew had been turning out to be:

SEPTEMBER 19, 2007

I would like to forget the time my brother's dog died. We have [sic] only had him for a month, then, he mystieriosly [sic] passed.

My brother was so grieved about his death that I wish I could have been the one to find our dead dog. Me and my dad disposed of his body, so my brother could take time to recover over his loss. It's been over a month since he's been gone, and I think my brother will be all right. The dog wasn't our only dog so it's not like he doesn't have a dog now.

Another entry reveals how important music was in Matthew's life:

NOVEMBER 13, 2007

Something I would never sell would be my old acustic [sic] guitar. My guitar has always been there for me and has never let me down. It was given to me by my former pastor and that is the most important reason why I will never sell it for any amount of money. I would hate to see it go and would miss it dearly.

Matthew was a natural musician. He taught himself how to play the guitar and sat on the platform at church, playing every Sunday. Penny was teaching him piano, and he was a quick student. But he was best known for his harmonica playing.

We had bought him a harmonica when he was about ten years old. I play a little, so I showed him a few things. But Matthew picked it up quickly and took it far beyond anything I had taught him.

Just before Matthew's last Christmas on earth, he wrote this:

DECEMBER 14, 2007

To me the meaning of Christmas is to celebrate the birth of my Savior Jesus Christ. Every year my family and I get caught up in the buying and the giving of presents, but every 25 of December we forget about the presents and we thank God for sending His Son for our eternal life. The meaning of Christmas would not be fulfilled without my family and most important Jesus Christ.

Matthew cared about others and knew how to empathize with them, as he shared in this entry:

JANUARY 10, 2008

To me the Native American proverb "Never criticize a man until you've walked a mile in his moccasins" means don't judge somebody by the way that they may appear. One example of that is, a friend of mine may seem different, but if anyone were to see his life they might think differently about this person.

Matthew also loved the outdoors. Some of his greatest joys were riding our Kawasaki Mule around our property or shooting tin cans off the fence posts with his BB gun.

OCTOBER 18, 2007

My favorite thing to do is go fishing on a cool morning just watchin' the Sun come over the horizon. I love to fish because it dose [sic] not have much to it. I would usaly [sic] go to a nearby lake or just fish out of my own pond. We usaly [sic] go as a family to a lake or up in the Arkansas mountains. I love to spit sunflower seeds while waiting for a fish to take a bite.

Like his mother, Matthew had a tender heart and always seemed to think more about others than he did about himself.

FEBRUARY 19, 2008

I occasionaly [sic] commit an act of kindness, for example, I found a five dollar bill fall [sic] out of the pocket of someone and I could have taken it and they would not have known. I did the right thing and handed it to the person and to my surprise he handed it back to me. He said for doing the right thing I was rewarded.

Less than a month before he died, Matthew made it clear that he was a follower of Jesus Christ. I drew deep comfort from knowing that Matthew was certain of his relationship with the Lord.

FEBRUARY 7, 2007

In my life there was an event that changed my life for the good and every day I'm glad that I chose to do that. That was the day that I gave my heart to the Lord. I was 7 years old when I took this very important step and I can remember the date and what day of the week it was. More importantly I can remember how it felt to change my life. Without me done [sic] that I don't know what my life could have turned out to be. I thank God for my parents and most important, the Lord.

As I lay in my hospital bed and thought about Matthew and his kind and caring spirit, I couldn't understand how a good and loving God could allow my sweet, sensitive bear of a son to die such a horrible death. It wasn't fair. It just wasn't.

HOMELESS

I guess the best way to describe me during my hospitalization is emotionally numb. I simply couldn't cope with the shock of losing Penny and the boys, having my house burned to the ground, and hearing of Erin's arrest. So I pushed all those horrific truths to the back of my mind. I didn't want to think about what was going to happen in the future. But even in the cocoon of my hospital room, the awful reality found me.

Wednesday of that week, I experienced the first moment of pleasure I'd had since the murders. I felt stubble on my cheek and realized that I hadn't shaved since the previous Friday. I asked Mary to buy me a razor and some shaving cream. When she returned, I got up and washed my face and shaved. I didn't know it was possible for something so simple to feel so good. But that was also the first time I had looked in a mirror since I'd been shot.

My eyes were puffy and black, and my right cheek had turned a dark purple. The right side of my face was scarred, and the stitches stood out like stubby whiskers. I had to be careful as I shaved not to damage them or reopen the incision. But the warm water and soap on my face made me feel as if I'd gone to an expensive spa.

The good feeling I got from shaving and cleaning up was probably the highlight of that week in the hospital. I spent the rest of the time trying not to think about what had happened—or what was going to happen.

Reality finally hit on Friday, March 7, when a nurse came into my room and said, "Mr. Caffey, we've done all we can for you here. We're going to send you home."

The word *home* smashed into me like an 18-wheeler. I didn't have anywhere to go.

I dissolved into tears and began weeping uncontrollably.

CHAPTER 9

HOMELESS

My God, my God, why have You forsaken me?
Far from my deliverance are the words of my groaning.
O my God, I cry by day, but You do not answer;
And by night, but I have no rest. —PSALM 22:1-2

"ARE YOU SURE I'm ready to leave?" I asked the nurse.

I was still crying, but I'd calmed down enough to talk.

Even though I had known the hospital would eventually release me, I'd never talked with anyone—not even family members—about what I would do after I got out. I had just tried to make it through one day at a time. I hadn't even allowed myself to think about life outside the hospital. So when the time to be released came, the idea caught me totally off guard.

"Yes, you're ready," the nurse said. "We've done all we can do here. You can finish healing at home."

"I don't have a home," I said. "My home was burned down. I don't have anywhere to go."

Once more my sister Mary came to my rescue.

"Don't worry, Terry," she said. "You can come home with us, and I'll take care of you."

The nurse dressed my wounds one last time and gave me instructions for keeping them clean and dressing them myself.

"Here are some medications the doctor has ordered," she said, handing me three prescriptions: one for pain, one for depression, and one for an anxiety medication. "You'll need to start physical therapy in two weeks to help you regain the use of your arm."

A few minutes later a wheelchair arrived to take me out to Mary's car.

When I left the room, a crowd of doctors, nurses, and hospital employees gathered in the hallway to say good-bye and wish me luck. As my wheelchair passed by, a lot of them hugged me and told me they'd be praying for me.

I rolled through the front doors of the East Texas Medical Center into a totally different world. On the surface, it looked like the same world I'd left behind only a week earlier. It was a beautiful day. Bright flowers bloomed all over the hospital grounds. People were milling about in the sunshine. Everything seemed to be alive and thriving. But there was one huge difference in the world I was about to reenter.

My family was no longer there.

Mary and her husband, Mike, tried to cheer me up, to get my mind off everything that had happened, but it didn't work. No matter where I looked, I saw something that reminded me of what I had lost.

As we drove north from Tyler, I looked out the window and watched life go by. Some people were driving. Others were gardening or mowing their lawns. Some were going in and out of stores, spending their day shopping. As I watched them, all I could think about was that these people had no idea what I was going through.

None of these people has any idea that my world has been destroyed.

We drove by a school with children on the playground. As I watched some playing on the swings and others throwing balls to one another, I felt a crushing weight on my heart.

Matthew and Tyler will never play again.

I couldn't make my mind accept the reality that my boys were gone.

Matthew would never shoot another tin can off the back fence with his BB gun. He'd never climb into the Mule and drive his brother around our property. Tyler would never again fill his red wagon with dirt and pull it around the yard. He'd never play with Max, our black Lab, again.

As I thought about Tyler, tears streamed down my face.

TYLER

Tyler was our free spirit.

Although he was outwardly shy like his brother and sister, Tyler also loved excitement and adventure. He regularly pushed the envelope where safety was concerned, much to Penny's dismay.

We had a small pond on our property. Tommy Gaston, the boys, and I had built a little deck near it, where we could have cookouts. One day Tyler noticed a long "Tarzan" vine hanging from a tree near the deck. In no time he had gotten some rope and tied it to the vine in a loop, making a perfect handle. Then, standing on the deck railing, he grabbed the vine, leaped off the deck, and swung out toward the pond and then around and back toward the railing. He was having great fun until Penny saw him.

"Tyler," she called out, "that vine's going to break. Don't swing on it."

Just to be sure it was safe, I swung on the vine myself. It held my weight and didn't appear to be stressed, so I told Penny that if it could hold me, it could hold Tyler. He was just a little bitty fellow. As for his homemade rope handle, he had tied it so securely that even Tommy couldn't get it off.

Tyler would swing on that vine for hours and have the best time, but it always made Penny nervous. Finally, Tommy came to her rescue. He asked if he could set up a rope swing for Tyler in a little circle of trees right in front of our house. Penny thought that would be much safer, so one Friday evening Tommy came over and hung the swing for us.

Tyler wanted to try it out right away, but it was dark and chilly outside.

"No, you can try it tomorrow," Penny said. "Maybe it'll be a little warmer out."

Tyler was disappointed and came in only grudgingly.

The next morning I woke up early. Erin and Bubba were on the couch watching Saturday-morning cartoons.

"Where's Tyler?" I asked.

"Out on his swing," said Bubba.

I looked out the front window, and there was Tyler, swinging on his new swing—in his underwear. It was a cold morning, probably only about thirty-nine or forty degrees, but Tyler didn't seem to notice or care. He was having the greatest time on his rope swing.

I opened the door and called out to him. "Boy, get in here and get some clothes on."

He didn't want to stop. "But, Daddy, I'm having fun," was his only response.

That was Tyler. Free-spirited and living in the moment. He also had a quick wit and a wry sense of humor.

One of his favorite expressions was "Just deal with it," and he'd toss it out often. One afternoon he was helping me work outside. It was one of those days when things just weren't going the way I wanted them to. Finally I got frustrated and threw down my screwdriver.

Tyler just looked at me with a deadpan expression.

"Daddy, just deal with it."

As we rolled into the driveway of Mary's home in Leonard, Texas, I could almost hear Tyler whispering in my ear, *Daddy, just deal with it.*

I didn't think I could.

LIFE AT MARY'S

Mary and her family lived in a small, two-bedroom house with only one bathroom. Mary and Mike had one bedroom, and their two daughters, Courtney and Hannah, shared the other. I was so thankful that they were willing to take me in, even though they didn't really have the room. I was nowhere near ready to face life on my own. Because there were no available bedrooms, I slept on the sofa in the living room. I didn't complain. It was the only home I had right then.

My only concern as we drove toward their house was their little dog, Tootsie. Tootsie was a small-breed dog, and like many small dogs, she tended to be high strung and hyper. I wasn't sure how well I would handle it if I had to cope with a lot of barking. I didn't know if my shattered nerves would take the noise.

After we arrived at Mary's house and they got me settled on the couch, Tootsie came over and sniffed me. Then she gently climbed up on the couch and sat down beside me. It was almost as if she knew that I was hurt and needed to be cared for, because she never barked or made noise. The whole time I stayed with Mary and Mike, that little dog was my best friend. And without being able to speak a word, she brought me great comfort by lying next to me and letting me hold and pet her.

But although Tootsie was quiet, my first night at Mary's was anything but restful.

Mary's house was old, with hardwood floors and dark paneling. It was also drafty, as older houses tend to be. The wind whined and whistled through the windows as I lay on the couch. Everyone else had gone to bed, and every sound seemed to be amplified. I was alone and frightened. I tensed at every creak and groan.

The front door rattled in its frame, and my eyes shot toward it.

Was someone trying to get in? What if an intruder came in and attacked us? We were completely defenseless. We could all be killed.

I surveyed the living and dining rooms.

This wouldn't do. It was too easy for someone to get in. I couldn't rest if I didn't feel safe. I took a dining-room chair and wedged it under the doorknob.

That was better, but not good enough.

I got up and pulled a small end table in front of the door. Then I stacked another chair on top of it, and a stool on top of that. I kept piling furniture in front of the door until I felt it would be impossible for anyone to surprise me in the middle of the night.

Finally I retreated to the couch.

As I sat there, a cool draft blew through one of the window frames. I shivered and wrapped myself in a blanket.

But it was too quiet. I was convinced that every noise I heard was someone trying to break into the house. Someone coming to kill me.

I got up and turned on the TV. I tuned it to my favorite channel, The Discovery Channel, and set the volume up loud enough to mask the other noises. Then I lay on my couch and kept my eyes fixed on the front door.

I was afraid to go to sleep. The last time I went to bed at home and turned off the lights, I woke up to gunfire. I did not intend to let that happen again. So I didn't sleep; I kept watch.

The next morning, Mary gave me a strange look when she came out for breakfast and found me sitting up. Then she saw my makeshift barricade.

"Terry, are you all right?"

I shook my head.

She smiled. "It's okay to barricade the door at night if it helps."

It helped—a little.

The next morning, after Mary and Mike left for work and the girls went to school, I took out my prescription bottles. The direction on the pain-medication bottle said to take one pill. I took two or three. I doubled the dosage of my antidepressant and anti-anxiety drugs, too. Then I spent the day in a drug-induced stupor.

It was the only way I knew how to cope.

I didn't dare go to sleep at night, but in the daytime, the grief was overwhelming. So Xanax, Lexapro, and Zoloft became my friends. They dulled my grief and helped me sleep. At night, I built barricades and kept watch like a terrified soldier on the front lines of a hellish war.

The next day, I'd start all over again.

This is no way to live, I thought.

But truth be told, I didn't *want* to live. I had fought to survive the night we were attacked only so I could tell someone that Charlie Wilkinson had murdered my family. I had expected to die once I had done that.

But something went wrong. God didn't take me.

I had been shot multiple times. How could anybody live through that? Someone told me I was a lucky man. If one of the bullets had been a millimeter to the left, it would have severed an artery, and I would have bled to death. If another bullet had ricocheted a little differently, it would have penetrated my brain and killed me. Yes, indeed, I was lucky to be alive.

But I didn't feel lucky. My survival felt to me like a huge mistake.

I should have died with my family.

I wanted to die and join them.

I looked at the bottles holding my meds on top of the end table by the couch. There were certainly enough pills there to get the job done.

It was something to think about.

CHAPTER 10

SUICIDAL

Why is light given to him who suffers,
And life to the bitter of soul,
Who long for death, but there is none,
And dig for it more than for hidden treasures?
—JOB 3:20-21

DURING MY FIRST WEEK out of the hospital, my routine quickly became a habit. Every night I stacked chairs, stools, and whatever other furniture I could find against the front door. Then I retreated to my couch, turned on The Discovery Channel, and watched the front door. When dawn came, I medicated myself enough to allow me to sleep through the day. My entire world revolved around a sofa that was not much bigger than a coffin. I guess that was appropriate; my life had shriveled into a living death.

Physically, I was well along the road to recovery. My right arm was still in a sling, and that limited me somewhat. I found it difficult to put on a shirt or a jacket. But these were minor aggravations.

My mind and spirit were another matter.

I'd always been told that God never gave us burdens too heavy to bear. Now I wasn't sure that was true anymore. He had certainly laid a crushing burden on me, and I didn't think I could bear it much longer. I couldn't understand how or why a loving God would let something like this happen to my family. It made no sense. All things work together for good to those who love God? I couldn't see how.

I couldn't see any possible way that good could come from Penny and the boys being murdered. Losing them hurt so badly I couldn't stand it. I felt as if someone had reached deep inside me and ripped out my heart.

At night, sitting on that couch with nothing to do and nowhere to go, I found myself constantly confronted by the reality of my new "life."

I would never again hug Penny or hold her close.

Never again would I help her in the kitchen. Sip coffee with her at the kitchen table. Eat her home cooking.

Penny would never give me another send-off to work, as she'd done every day for nineteen years. She wouldn't welcome me back when I came home.

I'd never go fishing with my boys again. Or lie on the floor with Tyler and play with his Hot Wheels cars.

Matthew and I would never do another harmonica duet. Or go hiking together.

We'd never stand around the piano as a family and sing while Penny's fingers pounded out a song on the keyboard.

I'd never hold my grandchildren.

If all that weren't enough, there was Erin, my precious daughter. The sheriff's department had said that she masterminded this horrible crime, that she was behind it all. I refused to believe that. I would never believe it. But that didn't change the fact that she was gone too. Even though Erin was still here on this earth, I'd lost my daughter, too.

The load God had given me to carry was killing me.

I was a Christian. I believed in God. I had trusted in Jesus Christ as my Savior. I knew deep down in my heart that God was real, that He was out there. I'd even been planning to serve Him in ministry.

But now I felt as if God had abandoned me. I had stumbled through dark woods as I fled my burning house. Now my life was a dark forest of grief and pain, and I was still stumbling.

From my way of thinking, God had taken away everything and everyone who was important to me. Why should I try to go on living? I was only forty-one years old. I couldn't face another thirty or forty years of life without my family. So as I sat on that lonely couch night after night, I sank deeper and deeper into despair. And I began to think about ending my life.

I considered a number of options but dismissed most of them as unworkable. I didn't want anyone to think something was wrong and try to stop me.

My property was isolated. Better yet, it was so thick with trees that you couldn't see much from the road. I could go there and be relatively certain that I would have the time and privacy I needed. Besides, since I wanted to join my family in heaven, it seemed only fitting that I die where Penny and the boys had died.

Slowly the idea began to take shape in my mind. I would have to wait until after the funeral at least. This was partly out of respect for Penny and the boys and partly for practical reasons. I needed more time to heal before I'd be well enough to travel to the property by myself.

I didn't think about the impact my suicide might have on Erin, or

Mary, or Tommy and Helen. I knew it was selfish, but I didn't care. I just wanted to stop the agonizing grief and the fear.

I had made up my mind and had a plan. I didn't know exactly when I would carry it out. But one thing was certain: I wouldn't wait long.

CHAPTER 11

FUNERAL

I have eaten ashes like bread
And mingled my drink with weeping.
—PSALM 102:9

I DREADED THE THOUGHT of the funeral.

The service had to be delayed for two weeks because Penny's and the boys' bodies were still in Dallas for autopsies. That was just as well. It gave me more time to heal from the gunshot wounds. I was discharged from the hospital on March 7. If we'd had the funeral the next day, it would have been a lot harder on me physically.

Emotionally, the extra week probably didn't make any difference. Because of the fire, we'd need to have a closed-casket service. I wouldn't even get the opportunity to see my wife and sons one last time. I wouldn't be able to say good-bye—at least not the way I wanted to. But that's not the only reason I dreaded the funeral.

I would have to face a lot of people that day. Up until then, my primary means of coping was hiding. But at the funeral, I wouldn't be able to deny my grief. I couldn't curl up in a ball on Mary's couch and hide from the world. I couldn't escape. It was going to be an excruciating day that ultimately brought no closure. All the funeral would do for me was to remind me that when everything was said and done, I would have to start over. I'd have to begin a new life— one without my family.

I was in no shape to plan a funeral service. My pastor, Brother Todd McGahee, and others stepped in and took that burden from me. Someone donated the caskets and burial plots, and the funeral was held at Miracle Faith Baptist Church, where we were members.

The week before the funeral, Rick Rumfelt, a friend of mine who was also a pastor, brought Penny's parents up to my sister's to get my input. As we discussed the arrangements, I wanted to make sure that the funeral service would not be sad. Penny and the boys knew the Lord, and I knew they were in heaven.

"Just keep it upbeat," I said. "I want us to celebrate their lives, not mourn their deaths."

Other than suggesting some of the music and selecting pallbearers, I left the rest of the details and planning to Rick and to my pastor, Todd.

Because it was a long drive from Mary's house to Emory, where the funeral would be held, Penny's parents invited me to spend the night before the funeral with them. They lived only a few miles from the church, so I wouldn't have to spend a lot of time riding in a car the next day. I welcomed anything that would make that day shorter and easier to get through. So on Friday, Mary drove me down to Emory and dropped me off at Larry and Virginia's.

MY LONGEST DAY

Saturday, March 15, was a perfect spring day in North Texas. Sunny and unseasonably warm, with a crystal clear sky, it was the kind of day that demanded outdoor activity. Matthew and Tyler would have been outside early on a day like this. But in spite of the sunshine, my spirit was as dark as the day was bright. The moment I climbed out of bed, I wanted the day to be over.

A funeral is a sad occasion, but it is also supposed to be the time when healing begins and when the bereaved can think about moving forward. I expected no healing to come from this service, and I didn't want to move forward. I hadn't chosen this new life—the selfishness and cruelty of two young men had forced it upon me. And although I knew that many people would try to comfort me today, I didn't expect to finish the day feeling comforted.

About seven thirty that morning, I heard a knock at Larry and Virginia's door. The funeral was scheduled for one o'clock. *Who could be showing up this early?* I wondered.

A teenage boy about Erin's age stood on the doorstep, and just seeing him there lifted my spirits.

James Jones had been a member of our youth group a few years earlier when Penny and I served as youth directors at Miracle Faith. I had led him to the Lord at summer camp and then baptized him a little later. In the years since, this young man had become like a son to us.

It was something of a surprise to see him there, but I invited him in, and we sat down in the living room. After a little small talk, we just sat quietly.

James sat with me all morning, from seven thirty until it was time for us to leave for the church, and in those five hours he ministered to me more than he will ever know. He offered no eloquent words of comfort or wisdom. He just sat with me.

When it was time to get dressed for the service, I asked James to help me put on my shirt. My arm was still in a sling, and the surgery to remove the bullets from my shoulder had left me stiff and sore. Even something as simple as putting on a shirt was difficult.

As James helped me, he started to cry. Tears spilled down his cheeks as he guided my wounded arm through the sleeve. He wept as he buttoned my shirt and helped me finish getting dressed.

That morning, a sixteen-year-old boy gave me a master class in how to minister to grieving people. He did more just by sitting quietly with me than he ever could have done by offering words of comfort. James's tears spoke volumes.

Because Penny's parents lived so close to the church, we didn't need to leave until just a few minutes before the service. At about twelve forty-five, Larry, Virginia, and I piled into their car for the short drive to Miracle Faith Baptist Church. James rode with us and, at my request, would sit with the family.

"I wonder if the media will be there," Larry said as we drove along.

I certainly hoped they wouldn't be. The day was going to be difficult enough without the presence of satellite trucks, reporters, photographers, and camera crews.

Pastor McGahee had done everything he could to keep the funeral from becoming a media circus. When any reporters or news outlets called, he told them that the family wanted to keep the funeral private and that he hoped they would respect our wishes by not coming. We didn't even allow Penny's and the boys' obituaries to be printed in the local newspaper until after the service.

As we drove along, we passed a man mowing his lawn, other people out in their yards, children playing. More people going about their daily lives, completely unaware that my world had been destroyed. As we turned the corner and the church came into view, the sight took my breath away.

The church's parking lot was overflowing. Many more cars lined the road. No media in sight, but more people than I could ever have imagined. My heart was overwhelmed. I wondered if the church could even hold all the people.

To think all these people are here for Penny and the boys.

We drove under the carport at Miracle Faith's side entrance, where a wheelchair waited. I climbed into it and was wheeled into the building.

I heard quiet strains of country gospel music in the background as we rolled down the hallway toward the auditorium doors.

MEMORIAL

"I want to walk in," I said. "I want to walk in for Penny and the boys."

Someone helped me to my feet, and I walked unsteadily toward the door. We waited until the funeral director gave us the signal that it was time for the service to begin. Then he opened the door, and with someone on each side of me, I walked forward.

I had barely made it through the door when I saw three silver-gray caskets directly in front of me, lined up end to end in front of the platform.

My legs went out from under me, and I would have collapsed had it not been for those around me, holding me up. Larry and Virginia helped me to the front pew, where I sat down, crushed with grief. There I sat, only a few feet from my wife's and sons' caskets. The sight was absolutely overwhelming. It hammered home the awful reality that I had desperately been trying to force to the back of my mind.

Penny's casket was in the middle, and it held an 8 x 10 photo of her. Matthew was on her right and Tyler on her left. Photos of the boys stood on their caskets, too. Behind them, even the choir loft was filled with mourners.

Once we were seated, another country gospel song began to stream through the church's speaker system. Seconds later, Penny's voice filled the auditorium. I began to cry as I heard my wife singing and playing the piano. I knew the song well. It was a recording of Penny and The Gaston Family Singers performing a song called "Take That First Step." I could almost see her sitting at the church's piano as the words of that song drifted through my mind.

I hadn't taken any medication that day because I wanted my head to be clear when I met and visited with people. But I was so numb from grief and depression that I remember very little of what went on. My friend Pastor Rick Rumfelt gave the eulogy. He told stories about the family, and his tone and words were very comforting. Then Pastor Todd McGahee stood to deliver the main message.

I was so proud of Todd. This was a terrible situation for even a seasoned pastor to face—this was Todd's first church, and he had been a pastor for less than a year. But he managed to keep his message upbeat and triumphant. Several times he reminded the congregation that Penny and the boys were more alive right now than they were when they had been with us on earth.

One thing I do remember is what Todd said about Matthew. He read two entries from Matthew's journal, written only about a month before Matthew died. One was Matthew's opinion about what a perfect day would be like:

FEBRUARY 1, 2008

My perfect day would be when the sky is clear and the sun's shining and everything seems to come my way. Most of the time that is not so, but when days like that come along they seem perfect. I like pretty weather so that I can go outside and enjoy the [sic] nature. That would be my perfect day.

The other entry showed Matthew's musical side:

JANUARY 23, 2008

My favorite song is Sweet Home Alabama by Lynyrd Skynrd [sic]. Why I like this song is because it talks about home. I also like the rythem [sic] and ryme [sic] of country-rock songs. When I listen to that song I feel great and listening to the guitars in the song makes me want to learn more. I love that song.

When Todd finished his message, he announced to the congregation that they were going to end the funeral a little differently. Instead of allowing the congregation to file by the caskets and exit first, he asked the people to remain seated while the family said their good-byes. Normally, the congregation is dismissed first so that the family can have some privacy in their final moments with their loved ones. But it would have been too hard to sit there while hundreds of people filed by. Some would have wanted to stop and talk, and I was in no condition to talk to anybody. Besides, I didn't need privacy when I walked by those caskets. I was so overwhelmed by the sight that I was unaware there was anybody else in the building.

With Larry and Virginia supporting me, I stopped by Tyler's casket first, then Penny's, then Matthew's. I ached to see them one last time, to touch them, to tell them I loved them. But Charlie Wilkinson and Charles Waid had taken away that possibility when they set fire to the house. So instead, I stood at each casket and wept until I felt as if I had no tears left. My heart felt as if it would burst. When I left Matthew's casket, the wheelchair awaited me at the auditorium door. This time I sat in it willingly.

As they wheeled me out of the church and toward the car, I saw Detective Almon from the Rains County Sheriff's Department approaching. Mary intercepted him.

"I need to talk to Terry," he said.

She cut him off. "Now isn't the time for questions. He hasn't even buried his family yet," she said, exasperated.

"Tell Terry that I need to talk to him," he said.

When I called him back some time later, he said, "It's too late now. The judge has issued a gag order, and we can't discuss the case."

I never did find out what he wanted that day.

VISITATION

We buried Penny and the boys in donated plots at the White Rose Cemetery in Wills Point, Texas, about a twenty-minute drive from the church. Todd kept the private graveside service brief, just some Scripture reading and prayer. As I looked at their caskets, ready to be lowered into the ground, I didn't see how I was ever going to live without them.

We returned to the church as soon as the graveside service was over. Todd had invited everybody to come back at four o'clock for a time of visitation. I desperately wanted to skip it, to go back to Larry and Virginia's house and hide. I didn't know how I would get through those next two hours.

"You don't have to go, Terry," Virginia said. "Everybody will understand."

I knew that was true, but I shook my head. "I need to go. All of these people came out to say good-bye to my family. I want to thank them."

About three hundred people attended the funeral, and at least a hundred of them came back for the visitation time. I pasted on a smile and tried to meet and greet as best as I could. It was difficult, but I was glad I went. I saw people that I hadn't seen in nearly twenty years. Even people from a church in Garland where Penny and I attended had remembered and cared. That overwhelmed me.

One lady, Nelda Walls, had been a coworker of mine many years earlier. Penny and I were very close to her and her husband, Stanley.

They were elderly now, and Stanley's health was failing. It touched me deeply that Nelda would take the time to make the drive by herself and be with me. Two months after the funeral, I went to spend the night with them at their home in Merit, Texas. They had set up a hospital bed for Stanley in their living room, and I sat by his bedside as he lay dying. We stayed up all night reminiscing about the old days with my family and his.

Many who came to the visitation shared stories about Penny or one of the boys. I appreciated the stories, but I found it difficult to listen to them. Every story was another painful reminder of what I had lost.

When the visitation time was finally over, we returned to Larry and Virginia's house, and I decided to spend a few days with them before I went back to Mary's. The next day was Sunday, but I had no plans to go to church.

Back in my room, I took a lot of medication. Double and triple doses. Then I went to bed, hoping I wouldn't wake up the next morning.

CHAPTER 12

JOB

Shall we indeed accept good from God and not accept
adversity? —JOB 2:10

"I WANT TO GO back to the property."

Larry and Virginia were concerned. "Are you sure it won't be too hard on you?"

"I don't know," I said. "But I want to go back anyway."

I could tell from their expressions that they didn't think it was a good idea. It was Monday morning, only two days after the funeral and just over two weeks since the murders. Maybe it *wasn't* a good idea. Maybe it *was* too soon. I just knew I needed to go back there and see the place for myself. I wasn't even sure why.

Tommy Gaston agreed to take me. Four of us piled into Tommy's pickup truck that cool, overcast Monday morning. My former pastor, Wayne Wolf, and his son Justin joined Tommy and me. Were they there to provide moral support, or maybe to help carry me back to the truck if I was overcome by grief? I didn't know, but I was glad they had come.

My stomach churned as we turned up Rains County Road 2370. As desperately as I had wanted to go back and see where everything had happened, I was also horribly afraid. When Tommy pulled into the driveway, the sight of my burned-out house took my breath away. Some of the debris had already been removed, but remnants of heat-scorched sheet metal still lay scattered around. Some of the house's subfloor remained. Ground zero—the area immediately underneath and around the house—was charred and black.

I climbed out of the truck and walked onto the blackened piece of earth where my house had stood only a few weeks ago. I dropped to my knees and began clawing through the ashes and mud.

"Nothing's left," Tommy called after me. "We've already looked."

But I had to look anyway. I had to see for myself.

Maybe I could salvage something from the rubble. It seemed as if Penny and Matthew and Tyler had been wiped from existence. I had nothing left to remember them by. No pictures or videos. None of their belongings. I was desperate to find something—anything—that would help me remember them.

I only had one good hand to dig with, but I dug through the rubble as if I were prospecting for gold. The black soot and ash felt cool to the touch. Finally, I felt something flat and metallic under my fingers. I kept digging until I pulled a skillet from the scorched earth. I clutched it to my chest and began to weep.

Penny held this in her hands.

I knelt there a long time, holding that skillet and crying. Finally I set it aside, but only so I could start digging again. My hands were black, and my knees ached, but I kept clawing through the mud and rubble, looking for anything tangible that might connect me with my wife and sons.

I found a Hot Wheels car that had belonged to Tyler, a partially burned picture of Erin and Matthew, a horseshoe belt buckle from a belt the kids had bought me for Christmas just a few months earlier. I held each item I found and cried, thinking of the person it was connected to. Everything I found was damaged in some way, but I kept and treasured all of it.

After a while, Tommy and Wayne told me that we needed to be going. I didn't argue. I had pretty well exhausted my energy reserves. I kept my treasures with me as I walked back to Tommy's truck.

READING JOB

When I got back to Mary's, I returned to my nightly routine: building barricades and keeping watch until dawn. The Discovery Channel continued to keep me awake and masked any outside noises. In the daytime, I still double-dosed my medication and slept. One day I slept seventeen hours straight.

One night as I sat there keeping watch, Roger Pippin's words came back to my mind: *You ought to read Job. You have a lot in common with him.*

That was what Roger had said when he brought me a Bible in the hospital. I hadn't appreciated his suggestion. I had read the book of Job many times before, and I couldn't see how reading it now would make any difference.

I was so confused at that point that I didn't know what to do or believe. As I saw it, I hadn't turned away from God; *He* had turned away from me. Where was He when Charlie Wilkinson and Charles Waid broke into my house and killed my wife and sons? Why didn't He stop them? Why had He allowed them to destroy everything I had? Why had He allowed Penny, Matthew, and Tyler to suffer such terrible deaths?

I didn't believe the Bible had any answers for me. Or at least I didn't want the answers I might find there. Nevertheless, when I moved in with Mary and her family, I brought Roger's Bible with me. It sat at the end of the couch at the top of a cardboard box that contained all my worldly possessions.

Night after night as I sat with the door barricaded and The Discovery Channel providing background noise, Roger's words began to nag at me. I tried to ignore the idea, but I couldn't get it out of my head. Finally, I picked up the Bible and opened it to Job.

This time, that book grabbed me as it never had before. In rapid-fire, almost machine-gun fashion, Job loses all of his wealth. One breathless, disheveled servant after another rushes into his home to deliver bad news. The Bible doesn't record Job's response to any of the earlier reports. Then, in what must have been the most crushing blow of all, a servant bursts in and tells Job that all of his children have died in a tragic accident.

At that point Job rises, tears his clothes, and says, "Naked I came from my mother's womb, and naked I shall return there. The LORD gave and the LORD has taken away. Blessed be the name of the LORD" (Job 1:21).

That statement startled me. How could Job praise God after losing everything?

I continued reading as Job loses his health and yet maintains his integrity and commitment to God. When his wife tells him to curse God and die, he responds, "Shall we indeed accept good from God and not accept adversity?" (Job 2:10).

Job almost seemed too spiritual for his own good. I wasn't sure I could identify with this man after all. In my opinion, to affirm God's goodness and sovereignty after facing such loss was superhuman.

And then I read chapter 3: "Afterward Job opened his mouth and cursed the day of his birth. . . . 'Why did I not die at birth, come forth from the womb and expire? . . . For now I would have lain down and been quiet; I would have slept then, I would have been at rest'" (Job 3:1, 11, 13). A lump formed in my throat as I read Job's words. He was expressing the very pain that I felt.

Job's suffering finally gets the better of him. But he doesn't curse God; he curses the day he was born. He wishes he had died at birth because then he wouldn't be experiencing such terrible pain and sadness. As I read that chapter, I identified with Job in a way I never had before. Many times since the murders I had thought how sweet it would be not to exist, not to have to suffer such incredible grief. That's why I was considering suicide. It seemed the only sure way to end my pain and suffering.

I continued reading. Sometimes I had to brush tears from my eyes. Other times, I just had to stop reading and weep. I read Job as if I were reading it for the first time. More than that, with every page I felt as if I were living Job's story with him. Sitting on that couch in that dark and drafty house, I wept with Job. I hurt for him as I hurt for myself.

When Job's three friends show up to comfort him—and instead accuse him—I felt the sting of their reproach. Nobody had accused me of wrongdoing, but I had accused myself plenty: *Were Penny and I somehow responsible for what had happened? Were we bad parents? Had we been too strict? Had we provoked the attack? Was this God's way of punishing us?*

As Job continues his discussion with his friends, his protestations of innocence grow stronger. At one point he expresses his desire to present his case to God face-to-face: "Remove Your hand from me, and let not the dread of You terrify me. Then call, and I will answer; or let me speak, then reply to me. How many are my iniquities and sins? Make known to me my rebellion and my sin" (Job 13:21-23).

At another point Job practically demands that God give him an audience. Job hasn't lost his faith, but he clearly wants to understand what is going on. Near the end of the book he cries out, "Oh, that I had one to hear me! Here is my mark. Oh, that the Almighty would answer me, that my Prosecutor had written a book!" (Job 31:35, NKJV).

That was exactly how I felt.

I wanted to understand why God had allowed such awful things to happen to Penny and the boys. I wanted to know what purpose such evil could serve. How could any good possibly come from it? *I wanted God to explain Himself.*

I read on.

God does grant Job a hearing, but the meeting doesn't go quite the way Job had planned. Instead of answering Job's questions and explaining why he was suffering, God confronts him with a series of impossible-to-answer questions. God asks if Job understands how the earth was created: "Where were you when I laid the foundation of the earth? Tell Me, if you have understanding, who set its measurements? Since you know. Or who stretched the line on it? On what were its bases sunk? Or who laid its cornerstone, when the morning stars sang together and all the sons of God shouted for joy?" (Job 38:4-7).

Further, God asks if Job has the power to control the universe: "Can you bind the chains of the Pleiades, or loose the cords of Orion? Can you lead forth a constellation in its season, and guide the Bear with her satellites?" (Job 38:31-32).

God asks if Job has the power and understanding to give birds flight: "Is it by your understanding that the hawk soars, stretching his wings toward the south? Is it at your command that the eagle mounts up and makes his nest on high?" (Job 39:26-27).

The questions go on and on. And all Job can do is stand there, dumbfounded.

As I read God's cross-examination of Job, I realized that He didn't expect an answer. To answer yes to even one of those questions, Job would have to have been God. And that was exactly what God was getting at. By demanding that God explain His actions, Job was setting himself up as a judge over God, and God responded by showing Job His power, greatness, and sovereignty.

The message was clear: Job needed to trust God even when he couldn't understand what was happening.

After God's cross-examination, Job realizes that he has been out of line: "I know that You can do all things, and that no purpose of Yours can be thwarted. . . . I have heard of You by the hearing of the ear; but now my eye sees You; therefore I retract, and I repent in dust and ashes" (Job 42:2, 5-6). Job comes to the point where he acknowledges God's sovereignty, even in his suffering.

I wasn't at that point yet. I didn't know if I'd ever get there.

At the end of the book, God restores Job's health and prosperity and even gives him a new family. The thought of such blessings was the furthest thing from my mind. Right then, I'd have been happy just to be able to sleep at night. Nevertheless, as I read Job, I began to realize that God might somehow have a purpose in what had happened to my family and me. I didn't know what it was. But if Job kept going, maybe I could too.

From that point on, I put away any thoughts of suicide.

JUST LET ME DIE

Reading Job was a breakthrough, but I was a long way from "normal." I no longer wanted to kill myself, but I still wanted to die. Whenever I went to bed, I'd pray, "Please, Lord, don't let me wake up." Then I would go to sleep, hoping that when I did wake up, I would be in God's presence. I imagined Penny and the boys rushing out to greet me and my grief vanishing in a flood of joy. Instead, I'd wake up still hurting, still buried under a mountain of grief, still wondering why God had allowed all this to happen.

I figured that I would go on wondering. God never explained

Himself to Job. If God didn't give Job an explanation, why would I think He'd give me one?

Quite a few people had quoted Romans 8:28 to me in the weeks since the murders. I had heard, "God works all things together for good for those who love Him," more times than I could count. But if that was true, I wanted to know the why and how of it. I wanted to know why God felt it necessary to take my family from me. And I wanted to know why He'd made me go on living.

But God wasn't talking.

COUNSELING

I knew I had to talk to someone. So when Bryan, my boss at Praxair, suggested I get into counseling, I didn't argue. I wasn't comfortable with the idea of sharing my thoughts and feelings with a total stranger, but I knew that if I didn't get help soon, I'd either change my mind and go through with my suicide plans, or I'd go off the deep end and wind up hospitalized. I figured that I didn't have anything to lose by seeing a counselor.

Although I hadn't yet returned to work at Praxair, Bryan kindly set up an appointment with a counselor named Steve. Steve's office was in Greenville, so it was convenient and easy to find. Mary took me to my first appointment because I didn't have a car and my doctor hadn't yet cleared me to drive after my surgery.

Steve looked nothing like what I had expected. He was in his mid-to-late fifties, had a full beard, and wore boots and blue jeans. He was definitely my kind of guy. Steve told me that he was a Vietnam vet. He'd been wounded there and had nearly lost his life. I knew from then on that I could talk to him, because he had seen more than his share of pain and death. He had experienced horrific things and had managed to recover. If anybody could understand the horror I had lived through, I believed Steve could.

He began by assuring me that whatever was discussed in that room would remain in that room. Nothing I said would come back to haunt me. Then Steve encouraged me to start talking. Whatever fear I had felt at the prospect of counseling melted away in the calm, reassuring atmosphere of Steve's office, and I began to tell him what happened that unspeakable night.

As I talked, it all started to pour out. All the anger I felt at Charlie Wilkinson and Charles Waid came gushing out of me like water from a fire hose. The pain came out too. I wept as I told him about losing my precious family and how much it hurt to think about what had happened to them. I shared my confusion about the possibility of Erin's involvement and about how helpless I felt.

Steve was great. He commented occasionally, and sometimes he asked probing questions, but mostly he listened. I don't remember how long I went on, or even everything I said. All I know is that I felt as if someone had lanced a boil that had been poisoning me. When I left Steve's office that day, I could honestly say that I felt better for the first time since the murders. I was still a long way from recovery, but as I read Job and met with Steve, God allowed a little light to shine through the dark clouds that had covered my life.

CHAPTER 13

THE ELEPHANT IN THE ROOM

Just as a father has compassion on his children,
So the LORD has compassion on those who fear Him.
—PSALM 103:13

EVEN AFTER PENNY'S and the boys' funeral, I couldn't really begin to move on or to adjust to a new life because the story was a long way from finished. During the first two weeks after the murders, I hadn't given much thought to Erin's legal situation. While I was in the hospital, I was so wrapped up in my own grief and pain that it was easy to give in to tunnel vision and focus on my own problems and needs. And after I was discharged, keeping myself doped up with medications made it easier to remain in denial. The thought of my daughter being involved in the murders was simply inconceivable to me.

Erin faced three counts of capital murder. Her grandmother Virginia went with her for her first court appearance because I was still in the hospital. The judge set Erin's bond at 1.5 million dollars, which guaranteed she would remain in jail until the trial. Because she was only sixteen, she was held in the Hunt County Juvenile Detention Center in Greenville. I was glad for that, at least. Erin was little more than a child herself. I didn't want her locked up with hardened criminals.

The judge appointed William Howard McDowell, a third-generation attorney, to represent Erin. But even though he was court appointed, I was told that he was the best in the area. I still wasn't able to drive, so Mary took me to his office in Sulphur Springs so I could meet with him and find out about the case against Erin.

When I arrived at his office and his receptionist let him know I was there, Mr. McDowell came out to the waiting area and greeted me. I liked him instantly.

His office wasn't at all what I had expected. Instead of a dark, austere room lined with shelves of law books, the office was filled with NBA memorabilia. Quite the basketball fan, Mr. McDowell had team jerseys, balls signed by players, and even a life-size cardboard cutout of an NBA player. The casual atmosphere initially helped to put me at ease, but that didn't last very long.

When we had sat down, I asked, "What are they saying about Erin's involvement? And what are her chances?"

Mr. McDowell told me that it didn't look good but he would hire a good investigator.

"Erin *couldn't* have masterminded this," I said. "I know my daughter. She loved her family. She wouldn't have wanted us dead."

Then Mr. McDowell began to review the evidence against Erin.

Charlie Wilkinson, Charles Waid, and Bobbi Johnson had all identified Erin as the mastermind behind the killings. They said that she had been talking about killing us for at least a month and that she was angry because Penny and I were interfering in her relationship with Charlie. The only way to solve the problem was to get rid of us.

Even worse, all three said that they had tried to talk Erin out of it and had encouraged her to just run away. But according to their statements, Erin had rejected that idea. They said that she wanted her brothers killed because the older one would talk and she just didn't like the younger one.

This was not the Erin I knew.

I knew that she had begun to change over the few months she had been going with Charlie. And things *had* become tense at times. But I didn't believe for a minute that Erin was behind the attack on our family.

As Mr. McDowell continued to lay out the evidence against Erin, the room began to spin, and I felt as if I were going to vomit. Everything he said after that was a blur. I was still trying to come to grips with losing my wife and two sons. And now this attorney was asking me to face the possibility that my daughter not only was involved in the murders but also had instigated them. It was just too much to take in. When I left his office, I felt as confused as I had when I first arrived.

Mr. McDowell offered a final word of caution for when I went to visit Erin: "Don't discuss the case with her," he said.

THE FIRST VISIT

The Hunt County Juvenile Detention Center permitted three visits and two fifteen-minute phone calls per week. Larry and Virginia had already gone to see Erin a few times. But it was several weeks before I was well enough to go for a visit.

Finally, I was able to make the forty-minute trip to Greenville to visit my daughter. Initially, I had to wait outside with a group of other parents who had come to visit their children. But eventually the authorities unlocked the building and allowed us into the waiting room.

I wasn't sure what to expect. What would it be like? Would Erin even want to see me? What would we say to each other? Finally they called my name and ushered me into the visiting area.

When I saw where we would be visiting, my heart sank. Before me was a long row of stools facing a thick Plexiglas barrier. In front of each stool was a telephone receiver. Erin and I would be only inches apart, but we would not be able to physically touch each other. I desperately longed to hug her and hold her hand, but that would not be possible. Worse, I wouldn't be able to talk to her about the things that were really on my mind.

There was so much I wanted to ask her: What do you know? Were you a part of all this? Did you really plan it? Did you know what they were going to do? But I couldn't ask any of those questions. They would be like the proverbial elephant in the room—impossible to ignore and so much in the way that we would tiptoe around them the whole time we were together. It would have to remain that way until her case was completely decided, one way or the other.

I sat down at the stool and waited for them to bring Erin in.

A few seconds later she came up to her side of the partition. I couldn't believe my eyes. On the other side of the Plexiglas window was my daughter, but she didn't even look like the same person. She looked awful. Erin had always been meticulous about her appearance. Her hair, makeup, and clothes had to be just so. Even when she was going with Charlie and let her appearance slip, she hadn't looked this bad.

She was wearing an orange jumpsuit. Her hair was oily and matted, almost like straw. She looked as if she had just gotten out of bed. Erin had always had clear, smooth skin. Now her face was dotted with acne.

But those things weren't what struck me the most. It was her eyes, her expression. Erin had always had a bright smile and a vivacious personality. Now her eyes looked dead, emotionless. There was no smile. She looked like a zombie.

We picked up our telephone receivers.

"Hi," I said.

"Hi."

"How are you doing?"

"Okay."

"Are they treating you all right?"

"Yes."

"Are you eating okay?"

She nodded.

"Do you have anything to read?"

This elicited a shrug.

This was killing me. My daughter was sitting not three feet away from me, and she was in as much pain as I was. I wanted to tear that window out of the way and get in there with her. We needed to be together. I wanted to comfort her. Tell her everything was going to be okay.

The longer we engaged in that meaningless conversation, the worse I felt. A host of questions roiled inside me, and I had to find a way to get them out without getting Erin or myself in trouble.

Finally I asked her, "Were we bad parents? Did we go wrong somewhere?"

Tears filled her eyes, and she shook her head. "No, you and Mama did a great job raising us. It wasn't your fault. Don't ever blame yourself for this."

I needed to know more, so I decided to risk using sign language.

Erin had been studying sign language with her aunt Mandy, and she'd picked it up pretty quickly. She and Mandy had done some sign interpretation for songs in church, and Erin had begun to teach a little to Penny and me. I didn't know much, but I knew enough to ask her, "Did you do this? Did you plan this?" I mouthed the words at the same time so she could read my lips, even if she couldn't understand my signs.

I expected Erin to respond the same way, but instead she just blurted out her answer: "No, Daddy. I tried to stop it, but it got out of hand." She was going to continue, but I motioned to her to stop. We had already said more than we should have.

That was the last time we even came close to addressing my most burning questions—*Was Erin involved? And if so, how deeply?* Early in April the judge issued a gag order. Any discussion of the case would put us both in contempt of court. So from week to week and month to month, our visits focused on the weather, jail food, reading material, general health issues, and other small talk. Our conversations were so limited and routine that I felt as if I could have missed a month of visits and we still could have picked up right where we left off.

One thing was certain: It didn't matter how Erin's trial played out. Her life would never be the same.

CHAPTER 14

LARRY AND VIRGINIA'S

The Lord will not reject forever,
For if He causes grief,
Then He will have compassion
According to His abundant lovingkindness.
—LAMENTATIONS 3:31-32

I HAD BEEN STAYING at Mary's house for about three weeks, but I was becoming restless. For one thing, I felt as if I were imposing on Mary and Mike. They were so gracious and supportive that I have no doubt they would have let me stay with them as long as I needed to. But because my bedroom was also their living room, I really felt underfoot. They needed to be able to get back to a normal family life, and that would never happen as long as I was camping out on their sofa.

Mary was instrumental in my surviving the first month after I lost my family, but it was time for me to get on with my life and let Mary and her family get on with theirs.

Another, more compelling, reason for my restlessness was distance. It was almost an hour's drive from Mary's place in Leonard down to Emory, where Penny's parents lived. It took even longer to get to the cemetery in Wills Point. With Erin's ongoing legal problems, I felt I needed to be closer to her and to the law-enforcement people in Rains County. Mostly, though, I just wanted to be nearer to Penny and the boys. If I was going to try to put the broken pieces of my life back together again, I wanted to be as close to home as possible.

Larry and Virginia had already invited me to stay with them, so I asked them whether the invitation was still good. It was. And so, on April 1, one month after Penny and the boys were murdered, I took my little box of personal belongings and moved back to Emory.

Larry and Virginia lived in a three-bedroom, two-bath double-wide with a wood deck across the front. I felt especially at home there because their living-room furniture had once belonged to Penny and me. We had given it to Larry and Virginia when we bought new furniture some years before. I found it comforting to sit on something that had once been in our home.

I also had my own bedroom at Larry and Virginia's. It was small, only about 10 x 11, but I wouldn't be in anybody's way. It had a twin bed, a dresser, and a small desk in one corner where I could sit and read the hundreds of sympathy cards that had come from people all over the world. It was overwhelming to think that so many people cared enough to take the time to write and encourage me.

The bedroom even had a small TV so I could watch The Discovery Channel.

It was also good for me to be with Larry and Virginia for another reason. All three of us had suffered a devastating loss. When I lost my wife and sons, they lost their daughter and grandsons. Now that I was living with them, we were able to comfort one another. Often we sat around and talked about how much we loved and missed them. Sometimes Virginia and I would just sit and hug and cry.

Larry and Virginia and I understood one another and shared that grief. Virginia, especially, could understand the double sense of loss I felt where Erin was concerned. When Erin was first held in juvenile detention, the judge had to hold a hearing every ten days to decide whether or not Erin's incarceration should continue. Erin's lawyer was going to ask that she be released into my custody. He had told me there wasn't much chance of that happening but also that there was no harm in asking. Virginia hoped the judge would agree, and she fixed up a room just for Erin. Virginia was devastated when the judge decided to keep Erin locked up. She, too, had almost had Erin back and then lost her again.

Moving in with Larry and Virginia also represented some progress on my part. Once I was at their house, I didn't feel the need to barricade the door anymore. I'm not sure why. Maybe I didn't hear as many noises. Maybe it was the counseling. Maybe it was a result of reading Job. Whatever the reason, my nightly routine changed. I still didn't get much sleep. I still doped myself up during the day, although not as heavily.

But there were still things that bothered me.

I was sitting with Virginia in her living room one day, and as we were talking, Virginia noticed that I kept glancing over at one wall. She was puzzled at first, and then she realized that I was looking at Larry's gun cabinet.

"Oh, Terry, I'm sorry. I wasn't thinking. Does that bother you?"

I nodded.

A little later I went out for a while, and when I came back, I saw that Virginia had put a blanket over the cabinet.

The next day, she and Larry moved it into their bedroom.

SAN ANTONIO

When you're not sleeping at night, you have a lot of time for reflection. Of course, I thought a lot about the last moments I had with my family on that Friday evening. But sometimes I'd find myself remembering other times—times when, much to Penny's chagrin, the children and I would unexpectedly find an opportunity to indulge our taste for adventure.

One such adventure had happened about four years earlier, on a family trip to San Antonio. We were driving south on I-35 when it began to rain so hard I decided it would be safer to get off the highway. We pulled into a deserted truck stop that had a large canopy where the big rigs could park. It was a perfect place for us to eat the lunch we'd brought while we waited for the storm to pass.

While Penny, Erin, and I were getting lunch ready, the boys went exploring. A few minutes later, they came running back shouting, "It's unlocked! It's unlocked!"

Sure enough, one of the doors to the café was unlocked. It was so clean inside that it looked as if the employees had just stepped out and never come back. We found a booth and ate our lunch inside the café.

When we had finished eating, Penny said, "We'd better get out of here."

But by then, the mischievous boy in me had awakened. "Let's look around first," I said.

We wandered around the café and the kitchen and worked our way through the rest of the building. Not one for adventure, Penny kept telling us that we should leave. The kids and I wanted to keep exploring. In the back, we found a door that led into a big area with large overhead doors. It must have been the shop for the big trucks. As we continued to explore, a cat came up to welcome us, so the kids shared some of their leftover lunch with him.

Suddenly I stopped and cocked my head. "I think I hear someone," I said. I hadn't really heard anything; I just wanted to frighten the kids—and I was successful. They got scared, and then Penny insisted that we get out of there.

I was just about to laugh and tell them it was only me joking around, but then *I* heard a noise and got scared too. We picked up our belongings and got out of there in no time.

We had a lot of fun on that trip and saw many of the sights of San Antonio, but the one thing the kids remembered the most, and talked about for years, was our thunderstorm picnic in that abandoned truck stop.

ERIN'S MARBLE

Now that I was living close to home, I started going back to my property whenever I could. I never went alone but usually would tag along with Tommy Gaston. As horrible as the memories were, I felt strangely pulled to the place where my family and I had lived. I made several trips with Tommy to look around and dig through the debris in hopes of finding something else to remember them by.

Tommy and others were working hard to clear away the remnants of the house and the other debris, so each time I went, the place was a little cleaner. On this particular day, portions of the subfloor still remained, but Tommy had hauled a good portion to the back of the property to be burned.

I stepped onto the ashes where the house had been and looked around. In the past I had had to get down on my knees and dig through the rubble, and whenever I found something, it was always damaged and blackened with soot. But this time I saw something gleaming in the sunlight. I walked over for a closer look, and there in the ashes lay a bright green marble. It was perfect. It looked as if someone might have just dropped it there. It certainly didn't look as if it had gone through a fire. It was so clean that I didn't even need to wipe it off when I picked it up.

As I looked at that marble and turned it over in my hand, my mind went back to a time many years ago, just after Penny and I had married. Her father, Larry, was the song leader at the church we attended in Garland. One Sunday he brought a basketful of marbles and told each of us to take a marble and to let it represent someone we wanted to pray for. Maybe it was an unsaved friend or relative, or someone who was sick. It didn't really matter, Larry said, but he told us to carry the marbles in our pockets or purses. Then, every time we reached for some change, we would feel our marbles and be reminded to pray for that person.

I looked at that perfect marble and thought of Erin. There were many unanswered questions between us, but one thing was certain: I would always love her and pray for her. No matter what she had or hadn't done, I would always care about what happened to her. I decided to keep that green marble with me as a constant reminder to pray for my daughter. From that day on, every time I reached into my pocket, I'd feel it there and ask God to protect her.

Erin was a sixteen-year-old facing the possibility of a life sentence without parole. I figured she'd need that protection.

CHAPTER 15

A MESSAGE
FROM GOD

Where were you when I laid the foundation of the earth?
Tell Me, if you have understanding. —JOB 38:4

NOW THAT I WAS living back in Emory, I had an amazingly busy schedule. There were follow-up appointments with the surgeons; Virginia
drove me to Tyler for those. I went to physical therapy twice a week,
and my right arm was regaining strength and function. I was allowed
to see Erin three times a week, so every Monday, Thursday, and
Saturday involved driving to the Hunt County Juvenile Detention
Center, visiting Erin, and then returning home. I continued to see my
counselor twice a week, and court hearings and meetings with Erin's
attorney were also sprinkled in.

I hadn't gone to church since the funeral, partly because I couldn't imagine going back there and facing all those people. It would be too painful. But I also hadn't gone back to church because God and I were still wrestling. Try as I might, I couldn't understand why He would take my family and leave me here. Why had I survived the attack that took Penny and the boys?

I had been so vulnerable that night in my house—shot at least four times and lying on the floor unconscious, wedged between the bed and the wall. Why didn't Charlie or Charles just finish me off? They had shot Penny, but they didn't stop with that. According to the coroner's report they had also attacked her with a knife, nearly decapitating her. Why didn't they do that to me? Why didn't they shoot me in the back of the head as I lay there immobilized on the floor? It would have been easy enough. Why had every bullet missed major organs and arteries even though they were fired at nearly point-blank range?

Even more perplexing was the fact that I had lost consciousness twice while I was on my bedroom floor. Why did I wake up after the first time? And when I regained consciousness the second time, the house was nearly engulfed in flames. How did I have the strength to get up? Why did I have the presence of mind to find my way to the bathroom, even though the smoke had virtually blinded me? How did I escape without a single burn when I navigated through that tunnel of flames that had been our bathroom?

When I finally got outside into the forty-degree temperatures, why didn't I go into shock? I had lost so much blood that I kept slipping in the puddle when I struggled to get up off the floor. My T-shirt and pajama pants were soaked with it. Why didn't I pass out as I hauled my wounded body through three hundred yards of brushy woods? Why didn't I pass out and drown when I fell into the creek?

I could think of scores of reasons why I should have died that night, but only one reason why I didn't: God had preserved my life.

He could have taken me at any time during or after the attack, the same way He took Penny, Matthew, and Tyler, but He didn't. He chose to let me live.

I wanted to understand why.

I didn't think that was too much to ask.

LOSING MY MARBLE

Although I'd made progress in the month since Penny and the boys died, I was still very fragile. One Saturday on my way to visit Erin, I discovered just how fragile I really was.

Before I was allowed in to see her, I had to pass through a security check, which involved emptying my pockets before walking through a metal detector.

I stood at the counter, and the officer gave me a basket for my wallet, keys, and loose change. When I pulled my keys out of my pocket, Erin's prayer marble came out too. It slipped through my fingers and fell to the floor.

I broke out of line and chased it as it rolled across the tile floor, headed directly for an office door. But just as I was about to grab it, it rolled under the door. I was just a fraction of a second too late to catch it.

I'm sure everyone else thought I had gone crazy, because I instantly became like a little child. I got down on my hands and knees and felt under the door with my fingers, crying, "My marble! My marble!"

The officer at the metal detector, a kind African-American woman, must have seen the panic in my eyes. She smiled at me. "What's wrong?"

Tears filled my eyes. "I lost my marble."

She didn't understand what I meant, so I explained to her why that marble was so important. I told her that it represented my daughter, Erin, and that it reminded me to pray for her.

The woman was very understanding. "The person who uses that office is gone for the weekend," she said, "but I'll see if we can find a key."

She made a few phone calls and talked to some other staff, but finally she returned, shaking her head. "That office is locked from Friday afternoon till Monday morning, and we couldn't find an extra key." Then she handed me a piece of paper with a phone number on it. "If you'll call this number on Monday morning, we'll try to get your marble. I'll leave word with someone so they'll know to look for it."

That entire weekend, I could think of nothing else but getting my marble back.

First thing Monday morning, I was on the phone to the juvenile detention center. They opened at eight; I was on the phone at seven fifty-nine. "Did you find my marble?" I asked.

I could hear the smile in the receptionist's voice. "Yes, they told us the whole story. That is so sweet," she said. "We've got your marble in an envelope. It's waiting for you anytime you want to come and pick it up."

I thanked her and told her I'd be right there.

I could have waited until I went for the next visitation, but I didn't. By now I had a rental car so that I wouldn't have to impose on others to drive me around. I hopped into that car and drove straight to Greenville. When I got to the receptionist's desk, I grinned and said, "I lost my marble, and y'all have it."

We both laughed. Then she handed me a white envelope. I didn't even wait to get back to my car. I tore the envelope open right there and dumped the marble into my palm. Then I wrapped my fingers around it, closed my eyes, and breathed a huge sigh of relief.

"Thank you so much," I said.

I went back out to the car, clutching my marble the whole way. I sat down in the driver's seat and opened my palm. As I looked at that little green piece of glass, the tears started to flow. That marble was my connection with Erin. Just as it had slipped so easily out of my grasp, I feared that Erin might be slipping away from me too. I wondered if I would ever get to hold her again. And in the privacy of my rented car I wept for my daughter.

AN UNMISTAKABLE ANSWER

I had come to believe that God might have some purpose in everything that had happened. But that belief wasn't helping in my daily life. I still felt as if my heart had been gouged out and a huge hole left in its place. It might have been too soon to feel any different, but the grief I struggled with every day threatened to overwhelm me.

I wanted to move on with my life, but I still felt just as unsure and blind and helpless as I had when I made the nearly four-hundred-yard trek from my house to Tommy's in the middle of the night: Stumbling blindly through pitch-black woods. Unable to see my hand in front of my face. Unable to take a step without wondering if I was going to bump into a tree or fall into a creek.

I needed some direction. I needed to know why God had kept me alive that night. I needed an answer, so I decided to drive out to my property and have a heart-to-heart with God.

I'm not sure why I decided that my property was the best place for that talk. I could just as easily have done it in my little bedroom at Larry and Virginia's. Maybe I just wanted to be close to where Penny and the boys had died. That place was my connection with them, just as the marble had become my connection with Erin.

Although I had visited my property several times with Tommy and others, I had never gone back there by myself. Tommy and Brother Wayne Wolf hadn't wanted me going out there alone for fear that I might become completely overwhelmed by grief.

But on this day, I knew that I needed to be by myself. I needed privacy. I couldn't pray, couldn't say the things I needed to say, with others around. So I got into my rental car and drove out Rains County Road 2370 to pour my heart out to God.

The sun sparkled through the tall, long-needle pines and broadcast bright strips along the earth. But the scarred ground where my house had once stood was a bleak reminder of tragedy.

I kicked the toe of my boot through what little rubble was left. Friends had bulldozed and cleared most of the debris weeks before, so there wasn't much left but dirt. I crouched down and ran my fingers through the soot, still hoping I might find one more memento, one more connection to Penny, Matthew, and Tyler.

Their voices rang in my ears.

Why hadn't I been able to save them? Why hadn't we had a gun? Maybe I could have stopped what happened. I might at least have saved the boys' lives.

I didn't understand any of this.

God could have stopped those boys from coming into my house and killing my family. He could have prevented Erin from ever meeting Charlie. No matter how I looked at it, God clearly could have kept all of it from happening.

The ground blurred, and I blinked away tears. I took some soot in my hand and let it fall through my fingers. In that moment, all the pent-up emotion, the frustration, the anger at God, welled right up into my throat. Maybe it wasn't right to be angry with God, but I couldn't deny my feelings.

My throat tightened, and bitter tears streamed down my face as I looked toward heaven and cried out loud, "God, why did You do this? I don't understand it! Why did You take my family and leave me here?" The anger and bitterness flowed from me in a way it never had before. "I need an answer! I need it now! I need it today!"

And that's when I saw it.

About fifteen feet away, a scorched piece of paper rested against the trunk of a pine tree, almost as if someone had set it there.

For a moment, I forgot my anger. Maybe it was a page from one of Penny's cookbooks or one of Tyler's picture books. I didn't care. Whatever it was, I would treasure it. I walked over to take a look.

I was amazed that the piece of paper had survived at all. It had been exposed to the elements for six weeks of North Texas winter and early spring weather. Several heavy thunderstorms had blown through. Many times, even houses didn't survive those storms, let alone a half-burned scrap of paper.

I bent down to look at it. The smoke and heat had blackened the edges and turned the paper dark brown. It looked as if it might fall apart if I touched it, but I had to risk it. Even if it crumbled to pieces, I had to pick it up.

I gently took the page in my hand.

As I read the first line, my throat tightened. For a few seconds I just stood there, a river of tears streaming down my face. But these were not tears of anger. They were joyful tears. Amazed tears. Awestruck tears. Humbled tears. They were the tears of a man who had just received an answer from God.

The first few lines of that burned page read, "I couldn't understand why You would take my family and leave me to struggle along without them. And I guess I still don't totally understand that part of it. But I *do* believe that You're sovereign; You're in control."

I fell to my knees and wept before God, thanking Him for caring enough to remind me that in the midst of the horrible tragedy I was living through, He was still there. And He had everything under control.

When Job asked God for an answer, God met him where he was. And although God never gave Job an explanation for His actions, He did give him a clear answer. He said, in effect, "Job, I am sovereign. I'm in control. And you have to trust Me."

And now, God had met me where I was too.

I believe that God preserved that single page for that exact moment. Out of the burned rubble of my house and everything in it, somehow God guarded a fragile piece of paper. He kept it from the fire. He protected it from bulldozers, trucks, and volunteer clean-up crews. He preserved it through several heavy Texas thunderstorms and high winds. And even though I'd already returned to my property five or six times, I never saw it until that day.

But when I was in the darkest well of grief, trying to understand what had happened and why, God allowed me to find that page. And through it He said, "Terry, I'm not going to give you an explanation. I'm not going to tell you why all this happened. But I am going to tell you that I am sovereign. I'm in control. And you have to trust Me."

In that moment, my joy in Christ returned.

d the beautiful Pleiades?
ose the cords of O n?
Wi   e one who contends with the Almighty correct him?
Let him who accuses God answer him

"I couldn't understand why You would take my family and leave me behind to struggle along without them. And I guess I still don't totally understand that part of it. But I *do* believe that You're sovereign; You're in control."

Justine's voice reverberated through his thoughts: *"Maybe God knew we needed you."*

"And I know that You've brought Justine and those children into my life. And they need me. Lord, You could have taken my life that day, but You spared it. And You've gone on sparing it. It doesn't matter what happens to me now, but if I can help them, please let me do it."

Thomas closed the drapes and stood alone in the dark room. For the first time in two years, he was at peace with God and with himself. He knew what he had to do. Justine and her children would be safe, even if he had to die to make sure of it.

Thomas walked over to the bed and flopped down on top of the bedspread. Almost at once he fell into a deep slumber.

Unretouched image of the actual page Terry found.

CHAPTER 16

FINDING PURPOSE

"I know the plans that I have for you," declares the LORD,
*"plans for welfare and not for calamity to give you a future
and a hope."* —JEREMIAH 29:11

I couldn't understand why You would take my family and
leave me behind to struggle along without them. And I guess
I still don't totally understand that part of it. But I *do* believe
that You're sovereign; You're in control.

THAT BURNED SCRAP of paper was a miracle—at least to my way of
thinking. Perhaps it wasn't a parting-of-the-Red-Sea or burning-bush
type of miracle, or one of those so-called miracles in which people
think they see the face of Jesus in an Idaho potato. And it probably

wouldn't qualify as a miracle according to a strict theological defini-
tion of the term. But, as a friend of mine later said, it was certainly an
act of God's providence.

I wasted no time buying a picture frame and putting the paper
under glass. I had no desire to make it into a shrine, but I did want to
preserve it. It was so badly scorched that it would easily crumble if I
handled the paper itself too much. But I needed to handle it. I needed
to read it carefully. I wanted to digest every word.

When I found the page, I had read only the first line. Then I'd
started crying, and my eyes were so blurred with tears that I couldn't
make out much more. Back in my bedroom, I began to read it more
closely. I'd already received a wonderful message from God in just the
first three sentences. I wanted to see what else, if anything, might be
there for me.

I didn't recognize the book the page had come from. It appeared
to be a novel or story of some kind. Unfortunately, the edges of the
page were burned, and all the identifying information had been lost.
The book must have been one of Penny's—she was the reader in our
family—but what the name of the book was, I had no idea.

Near the top of the page, above the lines I'd first read, I noticed
four incomplete lines that trailed off into the blackened edges. They
were formatted differently from the rest of the text, as if they were
poetry. I recognized them almost instantly as lines from the book
of Job.

The first line read, " . . . the beautiful Pleiades?"

On the next line, " . . . ose the cords of Orion?"

I'd read Job so much recently that I had no difficulty identifying
the passage. Those lines were from Job 38:31 (NIV), "Can you bind
the beautiful Pleiades? Can you loose the cords of Orion?"

The next two lines, also from Job, were more complete.

" . . . one who contends with the Almighty correct him?

"Let him who accuses God answer him!"

Those words were from Job 40:2 (NIV), "Will the one who contends with the Almighty correct him? Let him who accuses God answer him!"

In these verses, God confronts Job's self-righteousness and presumption in accusing God of treating him unfairly. God is saying to Job, "If you think you know so much, stand up and answer me." I couldn't help but feel that perhaps God was issuing a similar challenge to me. I certainly had challenged Him in my mind and heart.

The sentence following the lines I had read when I first found the page struck me almost as powerfully: "Justine's voice reverberated through his thoughts: 'Maybe God knew we needed you.'"

Quite frankly, the thought had never entered my mind that God had preserved my life because someone might need me. Ever since the murders, I had been so overwhelmed by my own grief and pain that I hadn't considered the possibility that I might be able to do something for someone else. I felt so weak and fragile. I couldn't imagine how I could be of any use to God, but there was always the possibility that God had kept me alive so that He could use me in some way.

In the next paragraph, Thomas, the central character, comes to grips with the fact that God still has something for him to do: "I know that You've brought Justine and those children into my life. And they need me. Lord, You could have taken my life that day, but You spared it. And You've gone on sparing it. It doesn't matter what happens to me now, but if I can help them, please let me do it."

One line in that paragraph really reached out and grabbed me: "Lord, You could have taken my life that day, but You spared it. And You've gone on sparing it."

I had no idea how God spared Thomas's life, but I knew for certain that He had spared mine. Humanly speaking, there was no reason I should still be walking around. Yet here I was. And although I had no idea what it was, God had a purpose for me.

The last two paragraphs on the page show how Thomas finds peace through submitting to God's sovereignty over his life:

> Thomas closed the drapes and stood alone in the dark room. For the first time in two years, he was at peace with God and with himself. He knew what he had to do. Justine and her children would be safe, even if he had to die to make sure of it.
>
> Thomas walked over to the bed and flopped down on top of the bedspread. Almost at once he fell into a deep slumber.

I finished reading that page and was no less amazed than I was the first time I'd laid eyes on it. I'm not the kind of person who hears the voice of God around every corner or is always going around saying to people, "God told me to do this." But I believed with all my heart that in that burned scrap of paper, I was holding a message from God to me.

As far as I was concerned, God was saying, "Yes, Terry, I took your family. And I know it hurts so much you can hardly stand it. But I'm not going to explain My purposes to you. You have to trust Me even though you can't understand what happened. I've kept you alive for a reason: There's still something I want you to do. Rest in Me, child, and let Me take you to where I want you to be."

As I looked at that page, peace flooded over me. God had indeed preserved my life, and I now believed that I could go on. He had a purpose for me.

My problem now was that I had no idea what that purpose was.

TYLER'S BIRTHDAY

Although the discovery of the burned page was a major turning point in my life and recovery, it didn't mean that all my grief and emotional pain automatically vanished. It is said that holidays and birthdays are the most difficult times for people who have lost loved ones in some way. I was about to discover just how true that statement was. In mid-April, I was facing a three-and-a-half month stretch that included Tyler's birthday, Bubba's birthday, Mother's Day, Father's Day, Memorial Day, Independence Day, Penny's birthday, and Erin's birthday. April 18 was Tyler's birthday. Tommy and Helen must have known how difficult it would be for me, because they suggested that we take a little trip to Broken Bow, Oklahoma.

It's about a three-hour drive from Emory to Broken Bow, so we got up early on Friday the eighteenth and headed north. We spent several hours sightseeing and enjoying the attractions. I welcomed the distraction but discovered that it wasn't so easy to put my son's birthday out of my mind.

We'd taken the kids to Broken Bow a few years earlier and had packed a picnic lunch. It started raining at lunchtime, so we decided to have lunch under a covered pavilion near one of the museums we'd visited. By the time we sat down to eat, it was pouring.

Tyler couldn't resist jumping in the puddles. After every few bites, he ran out into the rain and found a good puddle or two to jump in.

I could still see his utterly joyful face as he came down with both feet in those puddles, splashing water everywhere while the rain poured down around him. Penny's voice broke into my memories as well: "Tyler, get in here. You're going to get soaked."

Tyler would come back into the dry pavilion for a few minutes, but it wouldn't be long before he ran out again and took a flying leap into a new puddle. He was never one to leave a perfectly good puddle unjumped-in.

He would have been nine that day.

MOVING AGAIN

I stayed almost three weeks with Penny's parents, but I quickly became restless again. Although I had a very nice room at Larry and Virginia's, it still wasn't home. Just as my sister had been, Larry and Virginia were a great blessing to me when I stayed with them, and I'm sure I could have stayed as long as I wanted to. But I'm a private person and don't like to feel that I'm putting people out. I also knew that I couldn't stay with friends and relatives forever. Sooner or later, I would have to face life on my own.

I had talked about this when I was staying with Mary and Mike.

We'd discussed the possibility of my renting an apartment or a small house, but I didn't think I could manage it. The problem wasn't the expense involved. I was simply afraid to be alone. I didn't think I could live in a place that had a hallway or an extra room where an intruder could hide. I needed to be able to see the whole place at once. I finally decided that an RV would be the best solution. There would be only one room, so I'd be able to see all of it at once, but it would still have a bed, a kitchen area, a bathroom—everything I needed.

My sister's husband, Mike, found a thirty-foot RV on Craigslist for about seven thousand dollars. A friend put up half the money, and I paid the other half out of a special fund that had been set up for me.

We parked it behind Tommy and Helen's house. They had a lot of extra space, so the RV wouldn't be in the way, but I'd still have my own place. I'd also be living within walking distance of my own property. I could go there anytime I wanted without having to get in a car.

When I had moved my few belongings into my RV and sat by myself in my own place for the first time, I felt as if I'd taken one more step toward a normal life. I wasn't all the way back, but I was closer. I lived only a few hundred yards from my property now.

I wanted to move back there someday, but I wasn't ready.

Not yet.

ARKANSAS

God has a purpose for me, but what is it?

That thought had been nagging at the back of my mind ever since

I found that burned page on our property. There was one obvious answer, but I wasn't sure that I wanted to accept it.

It was mid-April, and that was supposed to be a time of great importance for me. Ever since Penny and I had married, I'd been involved in ministry one way or another. We'd been youth leaders at two churches, and I had spoken in churches and at camps. For quite some time, Penny and I had talked and prayed about the possibility that God was calling me to ministry. I approached Todd McGahee in the summer of 2006 and told him that I believed God had called me and I would like to be ordained. He brought my request before the church, and they set a date in April 2008.

After the murders, the ordination was postponed, and I hadn't given it any serious thought since then. It's hard to think about serving God when you believe that He's abandoned you. But ever since I found the page and became convinced that God still had some purpose for my life, the idea of ordination began to creep back into my head. Did He want me to serve Him in this way? Was I still called to ministry?

I was thinking about those questions late one Thursday afternoon when I went to visit Erin. Visitation didn't begin until seven o'clock, but I usually arrived about an hour early to get a place in line. Visiting was first come, first served, so there was usually a long wait before I got in to see her.

Because we weren't allowed to talk about the case, Erin and I spent most of our visits reminiscing and talking about the good times our family had had together. That evening our conversation drifted to our frequent family trips to Petit Jean State Park in Arkansas. We talked about how much fun we had and how it was our favorite getaway because it was one of the few places that didn't cost much more than the price of the gas it took to drive there.

"I love that place," Erin said. "It's so beautiful." A wistful look came over her. "We were going to go up there right before all this happened."

"Yeah," I said. "I remember y'all asking if we were going to hike down to the bottom of the canyon. And one of the boys said we'd have to leave Mommy behind 'cause she fell the last time."

We talked and laughed and cried together.

As I drove home, I found myself depressed and distraught, as was often the case after I visited Erin. I loved visiting my daughter, but each time I sat across from her with a pane of bulletproof Plexiglas between us, it reopened the wounds that were only starting to heal.

My mind kept going back to our talks about Arkansas and Petit Jean State Park, and I thought about how much fun we'd had and how special that place was to us.

I need to go up there for a visit.

The more I thought about the idea, the better it sounded.

As I drove toward Emory, I remembered a weekend we'd spent there. We had planned to go home on Sunday, and there was a church near Hot Springs that we wanted to visit. But we overslept on Sunday morning and wouldn't be able to make it to the church in time for the morning service. So instead, we all went up to the scenic overlook on the mountain, near Petit Jean's grave. It offers a majestic view of the Arkansas River valley.

On that weekend, we sat down together, near the cliff but safely behind the railing, and I read from the book of Genesis: "In the beginning, God created the heavens and the earth."

"Why do we like coming here so much?" I asked the kids.

"It's just so beautiful," they replied.

"Yes, it is," I said. "Just think: God made all this beauty just for us to enjoy. And we should always take care of it so that it will be here for others to enjoy, too, right?"

They agreed.

We had a wonderful time enjoying the beauty of God's creation as a family.

As I drove now, I remembered another trip where our more adventurous and mischievous sides came out. Somewhere I'd heard a legend about how, if you went to Petit Jean's grave after dark, you could sometimes hear her calling out for her fiancé.

One night when we were there, I told the kids about that legend. It was about midnight when I said, "Let's go up to Petit Jean's grave and see if we can hear her."

The kids were all excited and ready to go.

Penny reminded us that park rules said no one was supposed to be up there after ten o'clock at night. "I'm not going up there," she said. "And if a park ranger arrests y'all for trespassing, don't expect me to come bail you out of jail."

The kids and I decided to go anyway.

Our campsite was about a quarter of a mile from the gravesite, so we drove up to the ridge and got out of the car. After we'd walked around for a while, I stood a little ways off from Erin and the boys and started to make spooky sounds: *"Woooooooo."*

That was all it took. Erin and the boys were spooked, and we high-tailed it back to our campsite. As soon as we got there, the kids ran to Penny shouting, "We heard Petit Jean! We heard Petit Jean!"

I started to laugh, and Erin turned around and looked at me. "That was you, wasn't it?"

I just kept laughing and played dumb, as if I didn't know what she was talking about.

Petit Jean State Park, and that ridge in particular, were ingrained in my family's life and in my memories of them. I decided that I would go up to Arkansas and visit the park that weekend. It was a place of good memories, and it was a place where I believed I could talk to God.

I arrived back at my RV early in the evening, but I was restless. I paced around and tried to settle down, but nothing seemed to work, partly because I was still thinking about Arkansas and partly because I was still trying to figure out what God wanted me to do.

Was He asking me to continue with my plans to become a minister, or was He trying to tell me something else?

I tried to go to sleep, but I just lay there staring at the ceiling. Finally I decided that I needed to meet with God and find out what He was trying to say to me. And I knew exactly where I wanted to go to do it.

It was already past midnight, but I didn't care about the time. I threw some things together, hopped back into my rental car, and headed for Arkansas.

The drive from home to Petit Jean State Park took almost six hours, so I drove all night and arrived on the ridge just at daybreak. I went to the scenic overlook and climbed over the protective railing. There was a large boulder overlooking the cliff, and I wanted to sit on it as I prayed. To get to my perch, I had to jump a three-foot cleft between two rocks and climb up on the largest rock overlooking the Arkansas River valley.

The sun was just coming up when I sat down on that rock. Fog blanketed the valley, and mist swirled through the trees on the mountain as I sat there and watched the sunrise. I held my Bible in one hand and raised my other hand toward heaven. My emotions swelled, and tears rolled down my face as I poured out my heart before God.

For a while I just sat there and wept, but finally I said, "God if You want to use me, here I am. I'll do whatever You want me to if You'll just open the doors. But You've got to make it clear to me. What is it that You want me to do?"

As I sat there weeping and praying, I heard a car drive up. Up to that point I had been the only person there because it was so early. I glanced over and saw a maroon Ford Explorer in the parking lot. It sat there with the engine running for several minutes and then drove off. I didn't want to be distracted, so I paid no attention to it. I just continued to pray and weep before the Lord.

About five minutes later, the Explorer pulled back into the parking lot. But instead of stopping in a parking space, it pulled right up close to the walkway. A few seconds later a woman got out. She came quietly up the walkway, all the way to the railing I had climbed. Then she just stood there and watched me for a while. Again I tried to ignore her. I had come there to meet with God and seek His face, and I didn't want to be distracted.

Eventually, the woman turned and walked back to her SUV, and she and her husband drove off. It didn't occur to me until later that they might have thought I was about to throw myself off. After all, I was beyond the safety barrier on a rock overlooking a high cliff, and I was weeping. Evidently, though, the woman got close enough to hear me and realized that I didn't intend to jump.

I was probably on that rock for about an hour, but it was enough time for me to do what I needed to do. I had gone there to lay my life and heart before the Lord and to seek His face and His will for my life.

He had spared my life on the night when by all logic I should have died. I still didn't know exactly what He wanted me to do, but I trusted Him to open the doors as He saw fit, in His own time and in His own way.

I drove back to Emory with new resolve and purpose—that I would live my life for God's honor and glory.

CHAPTER 17

STARTING OVER

His anger is but for a moment,
His favor is for a lifetime;
Weeping may last for the night,
But a shout of joy comes in the morning.
—PSALM 30:5

I WAS DOING THE UNTHINKABLE—starting over. It had been only about two months since the attack on my house and family. Two months since my world had been destroyed. In those two months I'd experienced an incredible range of emotions and feelings. I had gone from almost total, suicidal despair to a grudging decision to live—although I prayed every night for God to take me. I'd gone from feeling that my life was over to believing that God still had some purpose for keeping me alive, although I still had no idea what that purpose was.

I began to read the Scriptures like never before. Before the murders, I had regular daily devotions, as many people do, but now I was devouring the Bible like a starving man. I spent almost every spare minute reading. I started with the book of Psalms, studying and underlining. I felt a strong kinship with David and the other psalmists. They were men who had known pain and who had also made God their stronghold in the midst of suffering.

After I finished studying the Psalms, I went on to the New Testament and worked my way through it repeatedly. I used to spend a lot of time watching TV. Now I used that time to read and study God's Word. Before long, there was hardly a page in my Bible that didn't have passages marked and underlined. But despite my newfound hunger for the Scriptures, I still battled depression. It wasn't unusual for me to pray before going to bed and ask the Lord to take my life during the night.

I knew that a rough road still lay ahead of me. The investigation was continuing, and I knew it wasn't looking good for Erin. I hadn't seen any of the evidence yet, but I knew that time was coming. Back in March I had met with Robert Vititow, the Rains County district attorney, and Lisa Tanner, an assistant with the Texas State Attorney General's Office. A capital case of this magnitude was too big for Emory, so the county had requested assistance from the Texas State Attorney General's office in prosecuting it.

Mr. Vititow and Ms. Tanner told me up front that they wanted to ask for the death penalty for Charlie and Charles, and I was fine with that. As far as I was concerned, I wanted to see them dead. In fact, at that point I would have been willing to save the state of Texas some money. All I needed was ten minutes alone in a room with each of them. I was so filled with anger and hatred toward Charlie Wilkinson and Charles Waid that I would have been more than happy to kill them. So I was fine with the prosecutors' plan to go for the maximum penalty with the men and with Bobbi Johnson, too. The problem was that they also wanted the maximum penalty for Erin. Because she was a minor when the crime was committed, they couldn't ask for the death penalty, but the prosecutors made it clear that they did want to request a sentence of life without the possibility of parole.

Erin was still in the juvenile detention center, incarcerated as a juvenile, but there was already talk of having her certified to stand trial as an adult. I hoped and prayed she would be tried as a juvenile, but I couldn't find out much because William McDowell, Erin's court-appointed attorney, seemed reluctant to give me any details.

At first, I couldn't understand why he was keeping me out of the loop, but then I realized that I was not only Erin's father but also one of the victims. Mr. McDowell evidently didn't want to risk confiding in me because of the possibility that I might be subpoenaed to testify against her.

I appreciated his desire to protect Erin, but I was also frustrated because I felt caught in the middle. Normally the prosecution represents the victim or victims of a crime, but because of my desire to support Erin, I found myself at cross-purposes with them.

Once again Bryan Roe, my boss at Praxair, came to my rescue, and the company hired a criminal defense attorney to represent me. It seemed strange at first. After all, I wasn't charged with anything. Why would I need a lawyer? But they explained that he was there to answer my questions and safeguard my interests.

Praxair didn't hire just any criminal defense attorney; they hired one of the best in the state of Texas: F. R. "Buck" Files Jr., from Tyler. I liked Buck from the moment I met him. He had close-cropped gray hair and a beard, and he was all business. The first time I met him, I called him "Mr. Files."

He shook his head and smiled. "Mr. Files was my father," he said. "I'm Buck."

Ms. Tanner thought highly of Buck and his skill as a defense attorney.

She told me that if she were ever in need of someone to defend her against a criminal charge, Buck Files was the man she would call.

That was good enough for me.

The legal process wouldn't start heating up for another month or so, but I was glad that when it did, I'd have Buck Files in my corner.

OCCUPATIONAL THERAPY

Once I had moved into my RV and was living next door to my old property, on Tommy and Helen's, it was time to begin preparing for my eventual move back home. I knew I'd have to move back there sooner or later, but I also knew that I couldn't go back to it just as it used to be.

The debris from the burned house had been pretty well cleaned up, thanks to Tommy and some other friends, but there was still plenty to do. For one thing, I wanted to clear away a lot of the trees. Before the attack, our house couldn't be seen from the road. I needed to change that.

I also wanted to clear a lot of the land between my property and Tommy's. That stretch was made up of mostly tall, long-needle pine trees and short, thick cedars. I loved the pines, and most of their branches were twenty or thirty feet high, with only the bare trunks down low. But I decided the cedars had to go. When I escaped from our burning house that night, the land between our properties was so thick with brush and cedars that I couldn't even see Tommy and Helen's house. When the time came to move back, I wanted all possible escape routes clear.

So as I began to regain my strength and the mobility in my right arm, Tommy and I started clearing the land between our two properties. Tommy brought his tractor, and a friend of his brought over a bulldozer. At one point we had cleared so much growth, both trees and brush, that we had a burn pile as high and wide as an average one-story house.

We also built up the driveway and leveled a pad where I would eventually move my RV. By my choice, the pad was directly over the spot where my old house had been, where Penny and the boys had died.

Some people thought I was crazy for wanting to move back there. For me, it was the only choice. I was not going to let Charlie Wilkinson drive me from my home and my land. It wouldn't be easy to move back there, and I definitely wasn't ready yet, but I was going to do it. I would face the fear and start my new life right where my old life had ended.

BACK TO WORK

Another step in starting over was going back to work. Ironically, this was one area where I had more going for me now than I did before the attack. I actually had two jobs I could go to. I could return to my old position at Praxair, or I could take the new job with The Henry Group that Ben had offered me the night before my family was killed. Although I was extremely grateful to Ben for holding the job offer open for two months while I recovered, I decided to return to work at Praxair.

For one thing, I would be returning to something I knew. Starting a new job would be stressful. I'd face a learning curve, new people, unknown pressures. Praxair was a known quantity. I knew my job, my coworkers, my boss's expectations. Plus, Praxair was willing to let me ease back into my schedule rather than immediately have to go back to a full-time routine.

I returned to work on Monday, May 5. For the first month, I worked only half days, and I was also allowed flexible hours. I was still going to physical therapy off and on and to counseling once a week. There were still court dates and meetings with attorneys, and I knew that I needed the freedom to take time off work for those.

Another area where Praxair was flexible with me was in regard to the need to be "on call." Although that responsibility was part of the job, Praxair gave me the freedom to decide when I thought I was ready to take on that responsibility again. I was most afraid of that part of the job because a call could come in the middle of the night and I'd have to go out. It was still difficult for me to go out at night, but my biggest fear was coming home to a dark RV.

I knew I couldn't face that yet. In fact, I honestly didn't know if I'd ever be able to go out at night again.

I continued to work with Praxair until September of that year, and I never worked another on-call shift.

One final reason I returned to Praxair was the way the company had stood by me throughout my hospitalization and all the hard times that followed. Bryan, my boss, had encouraged me to get counseling, hired my attorney, and encouraged me to keep going. Roger Pippin, my coworker, had visited me in the hospital and brought me a Bible. In fact, almost all my fellow employees had visited me in the hospital.

When the time came for me to return to work, Bryan even paved the way for me. He met with all the other employees and discussed with them how I wanted them to treat me when I came back. He told them that "business as usual" should be their approach. They didn't need to be afraid of what or what not to say around me. They didn't need to walk on eggshells. They just needed to pick things up where we left off.

My one regret about my return to Praxair is that Bryan was transferred out before I got back. I'd miss him. He was one of many people God used to minister to me and to teach me how to minister to hurting people.

BACK AT CHURCH

There had been one other step in the process of starting over, and it was one of the most difficult: going back to church. In the two months since the murders, I'd gone into my church only twice, and that was for the funeral and the visitation afterward.

For quite a while I didn't want to go back to church because I felt God had abandoned me. But over the past few weeks, especially since I'd found my miracle page, a desire had been growing in my heart to go back to God's people and fellowship with them.

It would be an understatement to say that I was nervous on April 27, the Sunday I went back. I got up that morning and couldn't manage to eat any breakfast. I had a cup of coffee, but nothing more.

Questions filled my mind. Would I be able to hold myself together, or would I collapse in tears? Could I even manage to enter the building? All these fears and more plagued me as I drove toward Miracle Faith Baptist Church that morning.

I deliberately arrived just minutes before the service began. I figured that would limit the amount of interaction I'd have to endure before I could sit down. When I got to the front doors, I paused, took a deep breath, and then plunged in, just as if I were jumping into a cold swimming pool. I wanted to get the initial shock over with quickly.

The instant I entered the church, I understood something of what the Prodigal Son must have felt when he came back to his father's house. There were no recriminations. None of the people looked down their noses at me. Instead, Pastor Todd and many of the people gathered around and welcomed me. Indeed, I felt like a long-lost sheep returning to the fold.

Soon we heard the sound of the piano playing, and we all took our seats.

I looked over to where Penny and I used to sit, about two-thirds of the way up on the right side of the church. I couldn't sit there. There were too many memories. Instead, I walked to the left side and sat in the very last row.

The song leader began the first song, and that is when it began to get difficult.

On the platform was an empty chair where Matthew used to sit and play guitar. I felt a lump form in my throat as that empty chair reminded me of what I'd lost. On the other side of the platform was the piano. Penny used to sit there and make beautiful music, but now someone else played. As the song service progressed, I began to sink back into the depression from which I had slowly been recovering.

After the service I walked back to my car, discouraged and overwhelmed.

I can't go back. It's just too painful.

I didn't think I could handle going to Miracle Faith every week and seeing so many reminders of Penny and the boys. So many memories of Erin and Charlie and the circumstances that had led to the deaths of my family members.

I went home certain that I would never return to Miracle Faith Baptist Church. But when Sunday rolled around again, I decided to go back one more time. To my surprise, this time was a little less difficult. Each week it got a little easier; the memories were a little less painful. I guess that's the way I had to approach life in general—one day at a time. Why not take church one Sunday at a time?

So, one Sunday at a time, one week at a time, I eased back into the life and fellowship of believers at Miracle Faith.

CHAPTER 18

MINISTRY

*[God] comforts us in all our affliction so that we will be
able to comfort those who are in any affliction with the
comfort with which we ourselves are comforted by God.*
—2 CORINTHIANS 1:4

HURRY UP AND WAIT seemed to be the order of the day where Erin
was concerned. Aside from routine court appearances, there wasn't
much going on in the legal arena. Because Erin was in juvenile detention, there was a hearing every ten days to determine whether or not
she should remain in custody. There wasn't any chance that they were
going to release her, but they had to go through the motions. I learned
not to get my hopes up. But I still attended the hearings, mostly so I
could be near Erin and encourage her.

There were hearings for the others, too. About every thirty days a court hearing was held for Charlie, Charles, and Bobbi. These were routine as well. I could have attended the hearings if I'd wanted to, but I chose not to go. I didn't think I could trust myself to be in the same room with Charlie and Charles.

The months of April and May were the calm before the coming legal storm. As I look back, I can see God's hand even in that, because He used those two months not only to prepare me for the upcoming trials but also to heal and restore me and prepare me for ministry.

Although God's hand in preserving the miracle page showed me that He was sovereign and in control of my circumstances, another evidence of His work in my life was the people He brought across my path. Never was that more evident than in how He worked through Rodney Gipson.

I was twelve years old, and Rodney was nineteen when we first met. Rodney began attending Hilltop Baptist Church in the Dallas suburb of Sunnyvale, the same church my parents and I attended. Rodney and I became acquainted with each other, but because of the difference in our ages, our friendship was casual at best.

As the years passed, I grew up and eventually left Hilltop when Penny and I married and began working with the youth at her church in Garland. Rodney got married too, but he and his wife continued to attend Hilltop. Over the years we lost touch with each other. In fact, almost twenty years passed before I saw Rodney again.

When he came to my dad's funeral in February, we reconnected. The age difference that had seemed so great when we first met really didn't matter now, and we hit it off. Rodney even called me during the next week to see how I was doing. After Penny and the boys were murdered, he and his wife, Sherrie, became involved in my life in a big way. Rodney called often to check on me and see if I needed anything. But one particular thing he did changed my life.

REVIVAL

About mid-May he called and told me that Hilltop Baptist was having revival services, and he invited me to come. Had it been a few weeks earlier, I might not have gone, but I'd already started going back to church, and that had broken the ice, so to speak. Rodney told me that the evangelist was a man named Andy Russell. Andy was a pastor from New Albany, Mississippi, but he was also very much in demand as a speaker, often preaching twenty to thirty revival weeks a year.

I decided to go, and I wasn't disappointed. Andy was a good speaker with a strong message. After the service I went to talk with him. As he heard a little of my story, he invited me to come visit him at his hotel the next afternoon.

The next day, Andy and I visited for a few hours. I showed him the pictures I still had of my family, and I showed him the burned page that God had used to turn me around. I shared with him the pain I felt at losing Penny and the boys and the almost unbearable depression I still struggled with.

Andy opened up and began to share some of his own struggles.

Then Andy said, "Let me ask you something. I'm preaching on Job on Tuesday night. Would you be willing to come and share your testimony with the people?"

His invitation took me by surprise.

"I don't think I could do that," I said. "I'd probably fall apart and be a blubbering mess."

Andy was undaunted. "Then come and be a blubbering mess," he said. "God can use blubbering messes."

I had no answer for that, so I agreed.

I went to Hilltop on Tuesday, my stomach tied in knots. I wasn't sure I could go through with what I had agreed to do. It had been only a little more than two months since everything had happened. It was still early in my grief. The wounds were fresh and still very painful.

I sat there waiting for my turn to speak. As the music service progressed, it was all I could do even to sing the songs. But finally, the pastor introduced me. I walked to the platform, dry mouthed and terrified. My hands shook as I held my Bible.

I held the picture of my family and the framed page.

There were only about 125 people in the congregation, but I felt as if I were speaking to a stadium full of people. I looked out over the congregation in the narrow church building and haltingly began to tell my story.

"When I lost my family, I felt that no one cared and that God had abandoned me. I was so depressed that I had planned to take my life.

"But one day I picked up the Bible and began to read the book of Job, and God spoke to me in a way He never had before. I saw in Job the same suffering, the same pain, I was going through. And I saw God's answer. God asked Job to trust Him even though Job didn't understand what was going on.

"Just trust me. That was God's message.

"And so I came to acknowledge that God might have some purpose in what had happened to Penny and the boys and me. But I wanted to know more. I didn't have to know why the tragedy had happened, but I wanted to understand what God was doing.

"So I went back to my property one day to have a heart-to-heart talk with God. And He answered me through this."

I held up the page.

"I was standing on the ashes of my burned-out house and crying out to God, telling Him that I need an answer and I needed it that day. And right then I looked and saw this burned piece of paper leaning up against a tree, almost as if God had put it there just for me.

"I picked it up and read the first few lines. This is what they said: 'I couldn't understand why You would take my family and leave me behind to struggle along without them. . . . But I *do* believe that You're sovereign; You're in control.'

"God answered me that day by reminding me that He is in control of my circumstances, even when I don't understand what is going on. I still don't know exactly why He saved me, why He preserved my life, but I do know that in His time He'll show me what He wants me to do. And He'll do the same for you. He loves you and will be with you in all the circumstances of your life, good and bad. You can trust Him, whatever happens."

To my surprise, there was hardly a dry eye in the house. My story, however haltingly told, was having an impact on those who were there. Later, when Andy gave the invitation, the altar was flooded with people who were in tears.

When I went home that night to my RV, I couldn't sleep. I was so excited that I sat up reading my Bible and praying till almost four in the morning. Was it possible that God wanted me to help others by sharing my testimony and telling them what He'd done for me? Second Corinthians says that God comforts us in all our afflictions so that we may share His comfort with others. Was God showing me that He wanted me to share my pain and struggles so that others could see how He had worked in my life?

If I had any doubts about that, they disappeared a few weeks later when Rodney Gipson and I went on a most unusual fishing trip—and never once went fishing.

FISHING TRIP

Rodney's wife, Sherrie, sent me a card letting me know that they both wanted to help and encourage me in any way they could. If I ever needed to get away, I could come and stay with them. She also mentioned that Rodney wanted to take me on a fishing trip to a place near Pittsburg, Texas. Rodney's fishing spot was actually a working cattle ranch that had several private lakes and cabins. He rented a cabin for us and packed up some tackle, and off we went.

We set the alarm for five o'clock so that we could get an early start on our first morning of fishing, but we never made it to the lake.

Rodney and I sat down at the kitchen table to have some breakfast, and it wasn't long before our discussion turned to Penny and the boys and Erin and all the things I'd been through over the last few months. But this time as I talked about it, something was different.

In previous conversations with my counselor or with other people, my focus had been primarily on my own suffering and pain and on how much it hurt to lose my family and how I felt abandoned by God. Now I found myself talking about how amazing and good God had been to me. I shared in more detail about the remarkable way God had spoken through the page I'd found. I shared not only how God had touched me through the book of Job, but also how I was beginning to develop an insatiable hunger for His Word. Rodney asked questions and probed, and I actually felt energized as I shared what God was doing in my life.

I told Rodney about how I'd been heavily medicating myself to escape the grief but that I felt it was time for me to throw away that crutch and trust God.

On and on we talked, through one, two, three pots of coffee.

Eventually, we noticed that it was past ten thirty in the morning and we had never gone out fishing. But we'd done something much more important. I had begun to realize that when I shared with others how God was working through my tragedy, I could actually see good coming from an unspeakably evil event.

Some time later, Rodney confirmed that he'd taken me fishing to cheer me up and encourage me but that I'd encouraged him more than I would ever know, just by sharing my story and showing him what God was doing in my life.

If God could do that with my friend, He could do that with others, too.

My mind went back to that misty, foggy morning when I'd sat on a boulder on the edge of a cliff overlooking the Arkansas River. I had told God that my life was His and that I'd do whatever He wanted, as long as He opened the doors and showed me what He wanted me to do.

Now I had my first answer. God had showed me what He wanted me to do. Now all I had to do was to wait for Him to open the doors.

As it turns out, I didn't have to wait very long. Word spread quickly about the testimony I shared at Hilltop Baptist Church, and I began to be invited to tell my story in other places as well.

One of the first places I spoke was the Van Zandt County Jail in Canton, Texas. After I finished speaking, a young woman named Jessie[1] came up to me and said, "I'm going to be getting out of jail soon. I've got a husband and two children at home, and I don't want to go back as the same person I was when I left them. I'm lost, and I need to be saved."

I took her aside and began to share the Good News of Christ with her.

I had Penny's Bible with me that day. Although it was scorched, it was one of the few things that had survived the fire intact. Inside was one of her bookmarks that had the Romans Road, a simple presentation of the gospel, printed on it.

Using that bookmark as a guide, I shared with Jessie how all of us have sinned and fallen short of God's perfect standard, and how the wages of our sin is death but God's gift is eternal life through Jesus Christ. As I worked through the verses that showed her how to place her trust in Jesus Christ, she hung on my every word.

A few minutes later, we knelt together, and she trusted Jesus Christ as her Savior. The jail chapel had a portable baptistry, so the chaplain and I pulled it out and I baptized her on the spot.

---

[1] Not her real name.

Before I left, I took the bookmark from Penny's Bible and gave it to Jessie.

"I want you to have this," I said.

She shook her head and brushed away tears. "I can't take this. It was your wife's."

"I know. But I think she'd want you to have it. Keep it to remember this day and the commitment you've made to God."

She thanked me as she and the other inmates returned to their cells.

As I watched her go, an indescribable feeling of joy filled my heart. I began to realize how God could use what had happened to me to turn people's lives around. There were so many hurting people in the world, and God could use my tragedy to help them overcome the trials that they faced.

As I was there in that jail, I also felt a connection with Erin. I couldn't be with her to minister to her personally, but I could share with women who were facing similar circumstances. I hoped and prayed that there would be people reaching out to Erin in the same way.

MOVING BACK HOME

It was time to go home.

I don't fully understand how I knew, but I knew that the time had come for me to move back to my property. In the last three months, I had been living with others, and I was so grateful for their help and encouragement. If it hadn't been for Mary and Mike, Larry and Virginia, and Tommy and Helen, I don't know what I would have done. They protected me, nurtured me, and encouraged me when I was overwhelmed with grief and pain. But if I was ever going to fully recover, I needed to be on my own again.

True, I was living in my own RV, but it was parked on Tommy and

Helen's land, and right by their house, where I could run if I needed a refuge. I needed to move it back home.

I knew that Penny, Matthew, and Tyler were with the Lord and that nothing was going to bring them back. But I still felt a need to be at the place where we'd spent our last night together.

So I set a date. I asked Tommy to help me move the RV back to my property on Saturday, June 7. That was going to be a difficult weekend because I had to speak in Brookston, Texas, the next morning. What would make it even more difficult was that June 8 would have been Bubba's fourteenth birthday. I suppose I could have put off the move a week or so, but I decided it was time to make the change. The longer I put it off, the more difficult it would be.

Would the memories be overwhelming? Maybe. But I was going to face them anyway.

God and I would face them together.

CHAPTER 19

HOME AGAIN

I will go in the strength of the Lord God.
—PSALM 71:16 (KJV)

FOR MOST PEOPLE, June 7 was just another day.

For me, it was a new beginning. I was excited, but at the same time, I was afraid. After three months and six days, I was going home. Not to the home I once knew. That, along with my family and everything I once owned, was gone forever.

Some people questioned the wisdom of going back to live at the site of such horror. How could I possibly move forward or begin healing from my grief when I was living in the very place where Charlie Wilkinson and Charles Waid had shot and stabbed my wife and sons and then burned down our house? How could I live in a place of such pain when I knew that Erin was being held as an accomplice in the murders?

Some people thought I was crazy, but they didn't understand.

I knew the danger. I knew that returning to my property could rip open wounds that now were only just beginning to heal. But if I was going to move forward, I had to start back there, the place where my family once lived. A place of good memories—and good sounds.

I missed the sounds of simple things, like the squeak of the dryer as Penny put in a load of wet laundry just before bedtime. I'd always ask her why she didn't start it earlier. Penny would say in her soft, sweet voice, "I'm sorry. I just forgot."

I missed the sounds of the kids whispering and giggling at night. "You need to be quiet and go to sleep," I'd tell the boys. They'd still giggle, only quieter.

I missed Penny lying next to me in our bed as we held each other and drifted off to sleep. I missed the gentle sound of her breathing. In these months after her death, I sometimes reached out for her in the middle of the night, only to find an empty place there.

It was the little things I missed the most.

Which would be stronger, I wondered—memories or fear? For that matter, would I even make it through the first night?

I couldn't answer those questions. All I knew was that I wasn't going to allow what had happened in the past to rule my life. I wasn't going to allow the actions of two young men to keep me off my property. If I was going to move forward, right there is where I needed to start.

So in a way, this was a new beginning, a new chapter in my life.

My heart pounded as I drove my truck behind Tommy Gaston's tractor. Even though I was moving only about three hundred yards up the road, I felt as if I were heading off on a long journey. As Tommy pulled my new RV up the narrow road toward my twelve acres, I knew that the only way I would be able to follow through on my decision to move home was with God's help. The words of Psalm 71:16 kept running through my mind: "I will go in the strength of the Lord" (NKJV).

As Tommy turned into our driveway, there was the sign that so many news programs had featured: The Caffeys, Joshua 24:15.

"As for me and my house, we will serve the LORD."

Those words still held true for me, even though they had been severely tested over the last three months. Like Job, I had lost everything: my possessions, my family, my health. Like Job, at times I had wanted to die. Like Job, I had questioned God's actions, asking Him why He would take my family and leave me to go on without them.

And as God did with Job, He answered me in a way I would never have expected.

Tommy's tractor slowed and stopped, and I rolled to a stop behind him.

As I looked over my property, I felt as if I were bringing part of my family back with me. I could almost see Penny standing in our doorway, as she so often did when I came home from work. Matthew out back, shooting aluminum cans off the fence. Tyler pulling his dirt-filled red wagon behind him—with more dirt on him than in the wagon. And Erin running out to greet me and ask how my day had gone.

I got out of my truck and stood there for a few minutes. I could almost hear the echoes of the kids' voices as they rode the Mule around the back part of the property.

Only time would tell if moving back here had been a good idea.

But, for now, I said softly, "Penny, kids, we're home."

FIRST NIGHT

Although I'd been sleeping alone in my RV for more than a month, this was the first night I would be really alone. I didn't have Tommy and Helen's house right outside my front door. No one could be there almost instantly if I needed help. I was back at ground zero. I was vulnerable again. And as the sun went down, I could feel the fear rising within me. It was going to be a long night.

The last time I'd gone to sleep here, someone had sneaked into my house and caught me totally unprepared. That wouldn't happen this time around. In fact, that would never happen again. I'd purchased a .9mm handgun and a license to carry a concealed weapon. Never again would I be caught unable to protect myself. When I went to bed, I made sure my gun was within easy reach.

I needed to get a good night's sleep, because the next day was going to be busy and difficult. I was supposed to speak at Brookston Baptist Church, near Paris, Texas. Also, it was Bubba's birthday. It probably hadn't been wise to accept an invitation to speak on a day that was certain to be difficult for me, but I believed that God had opened the door, and I was committed to going through with it.

I stayed up late, reading my Bible and praying, hoping that I would eventually become sleepy enough to drop off without too much trouble. Before I went to bed, I went through my new nightly routine. Instead of barricading the door, the way I had at Mary's house, I thoroughly searched the RV to make sure that nobody was hiding in any of the nooks or crannies. I checked out the bathroom and any other places where a person might be able to hide.

When I was convinced there was no one else in my RV, I checked my gun to make sure it was loaded and ready. I placed it by my bed, where I would be able to grab it quickly if I needed to. Then I climbed into the bed and turned off the lights.

I was pretty tired, so I figured that it wouldn't take me too long to fall asleep.

I was about to drift off to sleep when I heard something hit the window at the head of my bed. I was instantly on alert.

I heard the sound again, and again. It sounded as if someone were throwing pebbles against my window.

Thump, thump . . . thump. More pebbles.

My heart pounded against my chest. I checked to make sure my gun was still nearby.

Thump . . . thump . . . thump, thump.

My mouth was dry. I wanted to hide. Was someone going to attack me again, the way Charlie had attacked us a few months ago? Finally, I mustered enough courage to get out of bed and peer through the window blinds.

When I saw what was making the noise, I couldn't help but chuckle.

June bugs—a host of them—were flying kamikaze-style at the windows and the metal sides of the RV. They were the mysterious "pebbles" that had frightened me so.

Knowing the source of the mysterious sounds helped a little, but I still found myself attuned to every noise I heard, and I still felt compelled to investigate until I figured out what it was. I knew that I needed to pray and give this fear to God.

"Lord," I said, "I know that You are the one who protects me. Please give me Your grace and protection tonight, and help me to sleep."

When I had finished, I felt at peace and soon fell into a deep sleep.

BUBBA'S BIRTHDAY

Tommy and Helen had helped me get through Tyler's birthday by suggesting the impromptu trip to Broken Bow, Oklahoma. I'd managed to get through Easter mostly because that holiday focuses on the resurrection of Jesus Christ. Jesus Himself said, "Because I live, you will live also" (John 14:19). So even though Easter was a holiday, I took comfort in it because it was a reminder that Penny and the boys would one day be raised from the dead, just as Jesus was. Easter was a holiday of hope.

But as I awoke on Sunday, June 8, depression and sadness swept over me. My sweet, gentle son Matthew would have turned fourteen that day. I didn't want to drive to Paris and share my testimony. I just wanted to crawl back into bed and pull the covers over my head. *What had I been thinking? I should never have agreed to speak somewhere on Bubba's birthday.*

I wanted so badly to call the pastor and cancel, but I knew I couldn't do that, not this late. It wouldn't be fair to him or the church.

"God," I prayed, "I can't do this on my own. Please give me the strength to share Your word with those people." As I prayed, a verse popped into my mind, the same one I'd thought so much about the day before: "I will go in the strength of the LORD."

If I tried to do this in my own strength, I would surely fail. But if I relied on God's strength and His power, I could trust Him to use my words to touch people. And I could trust Him for the strength to get through the day.

So I got dressed and made the hour-and-a-half drive to Brookston Baptist Church.

I felt so weak and powerless that morning, but as I got up and shared what God had done in my life, He began working in hearts again. Shortly after the service was over, a tall man approached and put his arms around me. He wept as he told me that just a month before I lost my family, his son had been killed in an automobile accident. He said that he'd been struggling terribly since that day, but because of what I had shared, he had hope for the first time since his son's death.

"If you can go on after what you went through," he said, "then I can go on too."

I drove home that afternoon rejoicing that God was able to take my tragedy and use it to bring about good.

After I got back to Emory, I went back to my RV, changed my clothes, and then drove to the cemetery in Wills Point to visit Matthew's grave. It was a beautiful afternoon, and I must have sat there for a couple of hours, just talking to my son and praying and crying: *It isn't fair. We should be having a party right now. We should be celebrating your fourteenth birthday. All of us should be here: Mama, Erin, Tyler, and most of all you, Bubba.*

A feeling of heaviness had settled over my heart. I felt so empty, so alone. I went back to my RV, but I didn't feel any better there. A host of family memories flooded my mind, and with each one I felt more lost.

I decided to hang up my clothes and put them away, but I kept fumbling with my shirt. No matter how hard I tried, I couldn't make it go on the hanger correctly. Finally, in frustration, I threw the hanger across the room. Then I picked up more hangers and threw them at the wall.

"It isn't fair!" I shouted through my tears. "I want my family back! I need them! How can I go on without them?" I put my face in my hands and wept as if I had just lost Penny and the boys all over again.

This sudden, explosive feeling of grief took me by surprise. I thought I'd been doing so well lately. I was making progress. I had stopped taking the pain pills and the anti-anxiety medication. I had started a new life. God was speaking to me through His Word. He was using me to speak to others, and I was having an impact on their lives. What had gone wrong?

As I sat there, overwhelmed with sadness, I began to realize that even though all those things were true, it didn't change the fact that I had suffered a horrific loss. My family was gone, and nothing would ever change that. And no matter how God was working through the tragedy, the grief and the pain were still there and would continue to be there. I would have to work through those feelings for a long time. I would probably come to a point someday when the pain would ease—or at least become bearable—but I would always have to face the painful reality and live with it every single day. And the only way I would be able to do that was with God's strength.

I went to bed that night and tried to think of the good times we'd had as a family.

Once, when the kids were younger, Tommy was going to teach us how to make poke salad. You might call poke salad the Southern counterpart to the Japanese delicacy puffer fish. Just as puffer fish can be deadly poisonous if it's not prepared correctly, the pokeweed leaves are highly toxic but are edible if correctly prepared.

On this particular day, Tommy told the kids what to look for and sent them out to collect the pokeweed leaves. After a few minutes Erin came running back with an armful.

"Is this it? Is this it?" she asked, thrilled at her discovery.

"Nope." Tommy said, grinning. "What you've got there is an armful of poison oak."

I grinned as I drifted off to sleep.

CHAPTER 20

CRISES

I lay down and slept;
I awoke, for the LORD sustains me.
—PSALM 3:5

THE PAIN WAS ALREADY so bad that I didn't think it could get any worse.

I was wrong.

Matthew's birthday triggered a wave of discouragement and depression that went on for more than two weeks.

Father's Day was coming up, and I knew that would be difficult. But even before Father's Day I received a devastating telephone call from Erin's lawyer. On Monday, June 9, the day after Bubba's birthday, Mr. McDowell told me the prosecutors were going to request that Erin be certified to stand trial as an adult. A hearing would be scheduled to decide whether or not that would happen.

"Who makes that decision?" I asked.

"The judge will make the decision," replied Mr. McDowell.

"Then it's possible he could decide to keep her as a juvenile?" I asked, hopeful.

Mr. McDowell's tone was kind, but firm. "That won't happen," he said. "She'll stand trial as an adult. You can be sure of that."

For the past two months, very little had been happening as far as Erin's legal situation was concerned. Now that was about to change. I was terrified at the prospect that my daughter would have to stand trial as an adult. If the judge certified Erin, she would be tried in an adult court and face punishment in an adult prison.

Erin was only sixteen. She hadn't even had her driver's license for a year, and now she faced the possibility of a life sentence without parole, incarcerated with hardened criminals. In my mind, her biggest worry at her age should have been getting into trouble for staying out too late. I didn't care what they said about her; she was little more than a child. She wasn't ready to face adult life on the outside, let alone the harsh reality of prison life. How could she stand trial as an adult?

I felt as if I were losing my last family member. I had already had Penny and the boys taken away from me. Now the prosecutors wanted to take Erin, too. Once again the wounds that had begun to heal were being reopened.

I was back at work, and throughout the day the weight of this burden became heavier and heavier. For the first time in two months, thoughts of suicide began to creep back into my mind. What was the use in going on, anyway? I'd lost everything, and I was just kidding myself to try to believe that anything was going to change.

On my way home, I was so overwhelmed with grief that I knew I had to talk to someone about it. I don't know why, but I decided to stop at Larry and Virginia's house. They welcomed me in, and almost immediately I began to pour out my heart.

"I had to talk to you," I said. "I don't know what's happening. I was getting better and handling things pretty well, but ever since Bubba's birthday the grief is killing me again." I broke down and cried. "It just hurts so bad."

Larry and Virginia held my hands, and we wept together.

"I just want you to know how much I loved your daughter," I told them. "I couldn't have asked for a better wife, and the kids couldn't have had a better mother."

We spent a few minutes together, crying and asking God for His grace and mercy, and when I left, I felt better. One of the things I was learning through the grieving process was the power of tears. When the pain and sadness brought me to a breaking point, I would cry, and although my tears didn't change the circumstances, they lightened the burden and enabled me to get up and go on again. I had grown up in a culture that tends to look down on a man if he cries and considers tears unmanly. All I knew was that when I allowed myself to cry, it helped.

When I got back to my RV, a light rain had started falling. I opened the door and pulled the screen into place. Then I set up a chair and just sat there for a while, looking out at the sunset and listening to the rain gently pelting the roof. As I listened to the birds sing and felt the cool evening breeze blowing through the trailer, I began to view the world around me in a different way.

Life does go on.

I realized that even though Penny and the boys had died, there was still a world all around me, whether it was animals, or people going about their lives, or the rising and setting of the sun. The universe, the world, and life in general were continuing. That was what I needed to grasp. In spite of the way I often felt, the world didn't end when I lost my family. And as long as I was still alive, I had a responsibility to honor their memories by moving forward.

Even so, my depression that week was so deep that I didn't know if I could manage to do that. Was God still there? Was He still working in my life? Or had I just concocted all of this ministry stuff out of my imagination?

As I drove to church on Wednesday night, the burden was still heavy on my mind and heart.

"Lord, please speak peace to my heart tonight. Would You let me know, one way or another, that You're still there?"

When I arrived at the church, Brother Todd told me he had something for me and handed me a large brown envelope. When I opened it, tears filled my eyes. There were six cards, all from different parts of the country, all sent by people I didn't know. They just wanted me to know that they were praying and still cared about me. I had my answer.

Thank you, Lord.

NIGHT CRISIS

"I just wish it was all over."

Rodney Gipson sat across the table from me as we finished our dinner. I was so thankful for someone to talk to. Although I had good times and bad times, overall the depression that had set in with Bubba's birthday was showing no sign of letting up. I knew that a lot of it had to do with Erin's upcoming court appearance. Rodney had called earlier in the day and asked if I'd like to go out to eat. He didn't have to ask twice.

It still amazed me how God would take someone I'd known for twenty years but had never been close to and use that person to be such a blessing in my life. Even though I still struggled deeply with grief and depression, Rodney and Sherrie were like life preservers, and their house a lifeboat. They lived in Forney, about an hour and fifteen minutes away from Emory, so it took a bit of effort for him to take me out to dinner. But that didn't discourage him from reaching out to me. We agreed to meet at the Dairy Palace in Canton, Texas, about halfway between our two towns.

"I wish I could just make it all go away," I said. "The worst part is that I feel so helpless. There's nothing I can do for Erin. Nothing that will change her situation, anyway."

Rodney reminded me that God had everything under control.

I nodded. "That's the only thing that makes it bearable. I can rest in Him and trust Him to work it out for good."

Rodney and I connected so well that we had a habit of losing track of time. When we noticed the restaurant thinning out, we realized that it was already past nine o'clock.

"We'd better break this up," I said. "We both have to get to work early tomorrow."

Before getting into our cars, Rodney and I embraced.

"Thank you," I said. "Thank you for leaving your family to be with me tonight. I really needed to talk."

June days are long, and the sun had just set when I started the long drive back to Emory. By the time I drove down the country road to my property, it was almost ten thirty, and the night was pitch-black. It felt strange to be out in the country and away from the city lights. Strange—and frightening.

I never used to think twice about how dark it was out in the woods, but now I thought about it all the time.

I sat there for a few minutes with the engine running, my head-lights illuminating my RV. It looked as if a black hole had swallowed up the rest of the world. Beads of cold sweat formed on my forehead. I could almost hear my heart pounding against my chest.

I couldn't get out of my truck. It would be a walk of only about ten feet, but I would have to turn off the headlights and walk in the dark-ness the whole way.

I couldn't do it.

What was I thinking? Why did I move back to where my family was murdered?

Anybody could be hiding out there, waiting to attack me. And they would get away with it. Nobody would hear them. Nobody would know what happened to me until it was too late.

I knew that for a fact. It had already happened once.

I threw the truck into reverse and backed out of my driveway. Tommy and Helen Gaston were just a few hundred yards up the road. I could get their help. Tommy would come down and watch while I got out of my truck and walked into the RV.

When I got to the Gastons' place, it was dark, and their gate was locked. I had forgotten that they left on a trip the day before.

I've got to get ahold of myself. There's nothing out there to be afraid of. Nothing at all.

I drove back to my property and pulled into the driveway, but again I couldn't get out. After a few minutes I decided to drive to Brother Wayne Wolfe's house. He and his wife lived just down the road. They'd understand and help me.

But their house was dark too, and there was no car in the driveway.

I didn't know what to do, so I just drove aimlessly, killing time and trying to figure out a plan of action.

This is crazy. I can't drive around all night. I've got to go to work in the morning, and I need my rest. God, I have to go home. Please help me.

I pulled back into the driveway and cut the engine.

It's only a few feet. I can do this.

I threw open the door and ran as fast as I could to the RV.

As soon as I was inside, I locked the door behind me. My heart was pounding so hard that it felt as if it were in my throat. But I'd rest in a minute.

Before I relaxed, I had to conduct my nightly search of the RV. Because of its small size, that didn't take very long. First came a visual scan. Then I opened the bathroom door and made sure no one was hiding in there. The bathroom check also included a quick look behind the shower curtain. The only other place where someone could hide was on the far side of my bed.

Nobody there.

I sat down on my bed and waited for my heart rate to return to normal.

It was late, but there was still one thing I needed to do. I picked up my cell phone and called my pastor, Todd McGahee.

"Brother Todd," I said, "when you get a chance, could you come out here and pray over my land and ask God to bless it and take away my fear? I need Him to put a hedge of protection around me so that I can move forward."

I knew that the only true peace I would have must come from God Himself. But I also knew that I would have to continue trusting Him, even in the face of fear. He had promised that He would overrule my fear as I relied on Him: "You will not be afraid of the terror by night" (Psalm 91:5).

Nevertheless, I made sure that I would never again come back to a dark property at night. The next day I bought a security light, and after Tommy and I installed it, the area was lit up like a high-end auto dealership.

FATHER'S DAY

Since March 1, I'd managed to get through Matthew and Tyler's birthdays, Mother's Day, Easter, and Memorial Day. But the day I dreaded most was Sunday, June 15—Father's Day. More than any other, that day reminded me that I'd lost my family. In past years we'd go out to dinner, and the kids would give me presents, which they had usually made themselves. Penny would go out of her way to make the day special for me. We'd sit around the house, maybe gather around Penny's piano and sing together. Father's Day was a family day.

Now Father's Day had become one holiday that I would desperately like to forget. I wished there were a way I could just skip that day and miss it altogether. To make matters worse, I was still struggling with the depression that had begun on Bubba's birthday. And if that weren't enough, I had the added stress of knowing what was going to happen the day after Father's Day. On Monday, June 16, I was going to Buck Files's office in Tyler to meet with him and Lisa Tanner from the Texas State Attorney General's office. They were going to lay out all the evidence in the case, including the evidence against Erin. So all day on Father's Day, I would have to look forward to the next day, when I would hear why the prosecutors were convinced my daughter should be put away for the rest of her life.

That's what was running through my mind on Thursday, June 12. I'm not a superstitious person, and I don't believe in luck, either good or bad, but the next day would be Friday the thirteenth. That certainly seemed appropriate, because it was the beginning of the toughest four-day stretch I would face since the murders.

But once again, God sent people to help me through the entire weekend.

I was sitting alone in my RV on that Thursday evening when Brother Wayne Wolfe and his wife, Diane, stopped by out of the blue and asked if they could take me out to dinner. The Wolfes had been by my side since the day this all began. The night I was shot, they arrived at Tommy and Helen's house even before the sheriff's deputy and the EMTs.

We went out to a little fish place near Alba and had a quiet dinner. But when they asked me how I was doing, I had to be honest.

"Not too good, right now," I said. "I'm still pretty depressed, and I'm having trouble sleeping at night."

Brother Wayne and Diane didn't even hesitate. "Why don't you come spend the night with us?" Wayne said. Diane agreed.

I didn't need to be persuaded. They dropped me off at my RV, and I picked up a few things and then returned to their house. Wayne and I talked late into the night, long after Diane and their son, Justin, went to bed. Part of the time we talked about the things I was struggling with, but mostly we just enjoyed casual conversation.

Staying with Brother Wayne and his family definitely helped, but I still had a whole weekend to get through. Before I even had time to worry about it, God provided again. On Friday, Rodney Gipson called and invited me to spend Saturday and Sunday with him and his family. I especially looked forward to staying with Rodney because of where he and Sherrie lived. Forney seemed like another world to me. When I was at Rodney and Sherrie's house, I could put all my worries and fears away, even if just for a day or so.

On Saturday, Rodney and I went to the new Bass Pro Shop that had recently opened in Garland, right on the western shore of Lake Ray Hubbard. It was a magnificent place, and we had a wonderful time looking at everything. Later in the afternoon we went back to Rodney's house, and I did something that I never thought I'd do.

I watched golf.

Rodney wanted to watch the golf tournament, and I didn't have the heart to tell him I didn't like golf. So we sat and watched together, and believe it or not, I had a wonderful time. It wasn't so much the golf I enjoyed as it was the chance to relax, to take my mind off of everything that was going on. My life had become so hectic, so filled with activities, that I had no idea how tired I actually was. Between work, speaking, court appearances, meetings with lawyers, and visiting Erin three times a week, I wasn't getting much rest. A weekend with Rodney and Sherrie was as good as going to a retreat center. For at least that weekend, I was able to slow down and really rest.

On Sunday I went to church with Rodney and Sherrie, and we had lunch with Sherrie's father and the rest of her family. It definitely made my Father's Day easier to bear, but as the afternoon wore on, I knew I had one more stop to make.

I went home by way of Wills Point and stopped at the cemetery.

When I ordered the headstones for the cemetery, I wanted each one to reflect something of that family member's personality. That way, anyone who came by and saw them would know at least a little about my family. On Penny's stone, a piano keyboard was inscribed over her name. A music staff with notes floated upward from the keys. Matthew's stone also reflected his love for music, but in his case it was a guitar and harmonica with a staff and notes streaming out. Over Matthew's name I decided to add *Bubba*. Of course, I could imagine him up in heaven, rolling his eyes and sighing at the nickname he'd tried so hard to shake now set in stone. Tyler's stone featured a little wagon. It was the only thing he'd wanted that past Christmas, and he dearly loved it. Over Tyler's name was a Superman-type shield sprouting wings on each side, but with a *T* inside it instead of an *S*. Tyler was our flying superhero. Who knows? Maybe he really could fly now.

Tears blurred my vision.

"I just had to stop by and tell you how much I miss you. I love you so much. I always thought I'd go first and you'd be the ones burying me."

I knew they couldn't hear me, but somehow it made me feel better to talk to them, to tell them how much I missed them, how I wanted to be with them. But I also knew that God had His reasons for keeping me alive. Erin was one of those reasons.

Later that evening, I wrote in my journal:

I never thought that I would lose my entire family in one night and be all alone at the age of forty-one. Erin is all that I have left and I will stand by her side no matter what. I know she needs me, and I need her. I believe that God saved my life that night for a reason, and one of those reasons is to be here for her. I couldn't imagine her going through this without anyone, so I stand by her side and pray every day. There are a lot of questions that I have about that night, and some of those questions may never be answered in this lifetime. One thing that I do believe is that Erin loved her family and wouldn't want us dead. I believe they came that night, and things went bad very fast, and she had no control. So I keep trusting God to see us through, and that in the end He will get the victory and that His will be done.

I went to bed that night knowing that the next day—when I went to Tyler to see the evidence—would be difficult. I had no idea how difficult.

CHAPTER 21

CERTIFIED

He who dwells in the shelter of the Most High
Will abide in the shadow of the Almighty.
I will say to the LORD, "My refuge and my fortress,
My God, in whom I trust!"
—PSALM 91:1-2

I DROVE TOWARD TYLER, Texas, wishing I could be just about anywhere else on the planet. If ever I dreaded a meeting, it was this one.
Ironically, this was a meeting that I had requested, because I wanted
everything laid out on the table. I wanted to know what my rights
were, what the evidence against Erin was, and everything else that I
could find out. They asked if I would like to have my attorney present
to answer any questions I might have, and I told them I would.

We set up a meeting for Monday, June 16, at Buck Files's office. Lisa
Tanner and her assistant flew in, and I drove down to meet them.

I knew I was going to hear a lot of things I didn't want to hear. I wanted to know everything that had happened that night, for the sake of my own sense of closure. I needed to know who did what to whom. And I needed to understand how my daughter could possibly have been involved.

Immediately after the murders, Erin was unaccounted for, and the sheriff's personnel assumed that she had died in the fire. It was a few hours later, when a deputy went to the trailer of Charles Waid's brother, that they found her.

According to her story, two men had broken into her room and ordered her to get on the floor. Then they had taken her out to a car and kidnapped her.

When an investigator asked her what else she remembered, all she said was, "Fire."

Her pupils were dilated, and she appeared to be in shock, so they took her to the hospital in Sulphur Springs to get checked out. At that time, investigators assumed that Erin was a victim. When they questioned her at the hospital, Erin kept mentioning that two men were out to get her and that she needed to call her friend Charlie for help. She also said she was fourteen years old.

Once the doctors determined that she was all right, Larry and Virginia picked her up to bring her to Tyler to see me. Along the way, the police who were escorting them were notified that Erin had been implicated in the murders. They had Larry and Virginia pull into a parking lot, and they arrested Erin on the spot.

I knew that the three other suspects had implicated Erin, but I didn't know much more than that. I hoped this meeting would clear all that up.

We met in a conference room in Buck Files's office.

"Mr. Caffey, are you sure you want to do this?" the attorney general's representatives asked.

"Yes," I said. "I need to know what happened."

Lisa Tanner and her assistant laid out the evidence piece by piece. They told me how both Charlie and Charles had shot Penny and me and that later Charlie had come back and finished Penny off with a large sword, nearly decapitating her. They told me how Bubba tried to defend his family before Charles shot him in the head and neck. They told me how both men took turns stabbing Tyler in the back as he hid in his sister's closet.

Several times during the discussion, I broke down, and they asked if I wanted to stop.

"No," I said. "Go on. I want to know everything."

At one point, Buck Files left the room and came back with a box of tissues for me. But as difficult as it was for me to hear the evidence against the other three, it was crushing to hear what they said about Erin.

Erin's claim of being kidnapped didn't hold water.

Lisa Tanner showed me Erin's cell-phone records, which proved that she had made numerous calls to Charlie that night. She showed me interviews with classmates from Erin's school who said they had over-heard Erin and Charlie talking for almost a month about killing us. She showed me an interview with another boy Erin had dated. He claimed that even before Erin met Charlie, she had mentioned killing us.

In addition, all three of the other defendants—Charlie Wilkinson, Charles Waid, and Bobbi Johnson—claimed that the only reason they did any of this was because Erin wanted them to. According to them, Erin wasn't just involved; she was the mastermind.

As I drove home that evening, I felt as if I were in shock. Penny had always used to call me her hero. But I didn't feel like a hero. If I had seen this coming, if I had been able to prevent it somehow, then maybe I'd be worthy of being called a hero.

A husband and father is supposed to protect his family. I felt as if I had failed them all.

That evening, I prayed and asked God again for the grace and strength to get me through. I knew that I could make it through all of this only if I took things one day at a time. God was my refuge. Even though I didn't understand any of what was happening to me, I still knew that He was in control. I would trust Him through the pain and wait to see what He would do.

UNCONDITIONAL LOVE

A few days later I received a letter from Erin. As I read it, it lifted me up and gave me hope.

> *Dear Daddy,*
>
> *Let me start by saying Happy Father's Day. I hope you get this before then, but I don't need a date to tell you that you have been an awesome dad. You have done a great job, and not for one second do I think different. None of this was your fault. If anything, it was mine. I should have listened to you when you said you had a feeling about all this. You have always had a gift of knowing how someone is the first time you met.*
>
> *Anyway, I love you so much. I feel like I don't deserve your love and that I let you and Mama down. But in this family we stick together and I have always loved you, Mama, and the boys very, very much. I never wanted any of this to happen. I was just going with what he was telling me. He was feeding me all these lies. I got caught up in him, and I feel so guilty.*
>
> *I'm glad that you're here with me now. If it wasn't for you I don't know what would have happened to me. I love you. Even though this has happened, I still feel sad, but at the same time glad that I'm free from the pressure that was being put on me.*
>
> *I miss Mama and the boys! But I know where they are. I know they would be so proud of you. I am too. You're so awesome, going to preach all over the world. I mean, not that many teenagers have dads*

that are there for them. But I'm so proud to be your daughter. No
matter what anyone says, you have been a great dad and did a great
job raising me. No matter where I go or who I'm around, I will
never forget where I came from. And I dream one day of walking
together in our property, hand in hand. I do believe that that will
happen. Anyway, I love you, and happy Father's Day! Keep the faith.
God's about to show us His mercy!

Love, Erin

Tears filled my eyes as I read that letter. Hearing Erin affirm her love
for Penny, the boys, and me didn't change any of the circumstances.
She still stood accused of involvement in their murders. But something inside me changed that day. I'd heard the prosecutors' evidence,
and I couldn't answer it. I certainly couldn't disprove it. In fact, even
though I didn't want to believe it, it all might very well be true. But I
realized that day that I had to forgive Erin, and that forgiveness had
to be unconditional. I couldn't hold my forgiveness in reserve until I
found out whether or not she was guilty. I couldn't make it conditional
based on her level of involvement in the murders. I had to forgive her
completely and unconditionally, the same way God forgave me.

In just a few days Erin would face a judge who would decide whether
or not she should stand trial as an adult. I prayed that God would work
at that hearing. As I prayed, I remembered one Friday night many
years before, when Erin was a baby. Penny and I were going to go out
to eat with her parents. While Penny finished getting ready, I sat in a
rocking chair and held Erin. As I looked at this beautiful little child,
tears began to roll down my face. I thanked God for this wonderful
gift He had given us.

"I love you, little one," I said. "And no matter what happens, you
will be Daddy's little girl. I promise you that I'll always be your daddy
and I'll always be there for you."

Now, nearly seventeen years later, I would stand by her side and be there for her as she faced charges of capital murder.

No matter what, she would always be Daddy's little girl.

CERTIFICATION HEARING

On June 26, the day of the hearing, I picked up Larry and Virginia, and we drove to the courthouse together. Although I hoped that the judge would allow Erin to be tried as a juvenile, her attorney had already told me that wouldn't happen. So even though I didn't want to believe that she'd be certified as an adult, I was somewhat prepared for that outcome.

When they brought Erin into the courtroom, I was allowed to sit by her at the defendant's table. We hugged, but we didn't get to talk much.

The hearing was brief and to the point.

I took the stand and asked the judge to release Erin into my custody or at least to keep her as a juvenile. After I finished, the district attorney said that Erin was a danger to herself and to society. He also explained the horrific nature of the crimes and requested that Erin be certified to stand trial as an adult. After the district attorney had finished, the judge rendered his decision. As Mr. McDowell had warned me, it appeared to be a foregone conclusion.

"This court certifies Erin Michelle Caffey to stand trial as an adult."

It was over that quickly.

The bailiff came to take Erin away. I managed a quick embrace. "I love you," I said. "I'll see you soon."

We were both crying as they led her out.

I had been afraid for Erin because I thought that being certified as an adult meant that she'd be locked up with hardened criminals. As it turned out, that was not the case. Immediately after the hearing, Erin was taken to the Hopkins County Jail in Sulphur Springs and placed in protective custody. On one hand, she would not be in a cell with someone who might hurt her; on the other, she would be in solitary confinement until her trial, which was still months away.

That evening was one of the toughest I had experienced since the murders. I got in my truck and drove around for hours, hurt and bewildered. Any hope that I might have Erin back someday was slipping away. I felt so alone.

Would I ever have a family again?

CHAPTER 22

SONJA

*The LORD God said, "It is not good for the man to be alone." —*GENESIS 2:18

I HAD KNOWN Sonja Webb for more than eight years. We both worked in the home-health industry, and we had met at a luncheon marketing our respective companies' services to local physicians. At the time, she was working for Praxair, and I was working for Hometown Medical, a small start-up company. I'd worked for Praxair before going with Hometown, and that provided the basis for our conversation.

"I used to work for Praxair," I had told her.

"I know," she said. "They speak very highly of you over there."

"Yeah, I worked there for a couple of years before I branched off with these guys," I said, nodding toward the Hometown Medical display.

Other than a little small talk, our conversation that day didn't amount to much. Over the next eight years, I ran into her occasionally in doctors' offices, but all we'd do is say hello and go our separate ways. Eventually, I left Hometown Medical and returned to my old job at Praxair. But even though we were coworkers, our paths didn't cross very often. Sonja was in sales, and I was in distribution. She spent most of her time working on marketing and didn't often work from the Greenville office. I was usually in the field, delivering and setting up equipment.

After Penny and the boys died, Sonja, along with everyone in my local office, came to the funeral, but she hadn't been able to visit me in the hospital. She felt bad about that, particularly because everyone else in the office had made it to Tyler to visit me at least once. So shortly after I started back at Praxair, she stopped by and apologized.

"I'm sorry I didn't get a chance to see you when you were in the hospital. But I want you to know that I was thinking about you and praying for you."

"That's okay," I said. "I appreciate it."

Again it was a passing conversation, and then we went our own ways. But after I'd been back about a month and a half, she stopped by again.

"Do you have a minute?" she asked.

"Sure."

"I just wanted to tell you how much I admire your courage and strength and your faith in God. After all you've gone through, you're still serving God and using your experience to reach out to others. Watching you has made me realize that I need to get back into church. I've been out of church for several years now. I used to take my boys, and we were all involved. I need to get my boys back in church."

"Yes, you do," I replied. "And y'all are welcome to come out to my church anytime you want to. I know it's a little far from Wills Point, but we'd love to have you." Then I asked her, "Is there a church close to y'all that you could get involved in?"

"Yes," she said. "There's a little church near us that we used to go to, but we never really felt at home there."

"Well, you're welcome to come out and visit my church anytime."

It wasn't until later that I began to wonder if Sonja would have lunch with me. Praxair was doing a lot of restructuring at the time, and she was in the office a lot more than usual, catching up on paperwork. Even though we hadn't talked much, I'd enjoyed the few times I'd spoken with her. I didn't have any romantic inclination. I wasn't falling in love. But it had been so long since I'd sat and talked with Penny that I thought it would be nice to sit down and talk with a woman again. I knew that Sonja was divorced and had two sons, and I'd heard that she'd had a pretty rough time. I could talk to her more about church and ask her about her boys. It just seemed right to do that.

So when I saw Sonja a few days later, I asked, "Would you like to catch lunch sometime?"

I expected her to brush me off with "Oh, maybe one of these days."

So I was floored when she said, "Sure! How about tomorrow?"

We went to Chili's the next day and had a wonderful time. I don't even remember what we talked about, just that it was such a nice, relaxed conversation. I hadn't realized until I sat down with Sonja how much I had missed the companionship of a woman. Losing Penny had created a deep void in my life, but until that day at Chili's, I hadn't realized how deep.

When we got up to leave, I let her go ahead of me, and as she passed by, I caught a whiff of her perfume. That was the first time in almost twenty years that I'd noticed another woman's perfume. I'd been married to Penny and was completely devoted to her. But that afternoon I began to wonder if God might possibly bring someone else into my life. Not to replace Penny. No one could ever do that. But someone to be by my side. A helper. A wife.

A few days after our lunch at Chili's, Sonja invited me to her family reunion. It was going to be in Alba, and she knew that's where I lived. I thought it would be a nice change of pace, and I had nothing else to do that Saturday. I'd have just been sitting around at my trailer. We agreed to go as friends.

I didn't find out until later, but at the reunion many of Sonja's relatives asked her about me. She told them that I was just a coworker, a friend she'd invited because I lived nearby. It seems that quite a few of her aunts and uncles grinned and said, "You're going to be more than friends. You two just look too good together."

WHIRLWIND COURTSHIP

After the reunion on June 28, our relationship took off. Sonja and I began dating and spending more time together. Everything clicked between us. I met her two sons, Blake and Tanner, and was amazed at how much they reminded me of Bubba and Tyler. Blake, seventeen, was a big boy with dark curly hair and a gentle personality, just like Bubba's. Tanner was an adventurous nine-year-old, was very much like Tyler.

As it became clear to me that the relationship with Sonja was getting serious, I began to consider the implications of such a whirlwind courtship. One evening, I wrote in my journal,

I am trying to take it slow, but in just a short time of being around her I feel my heart giving in. She makes me feel so good, and when I look into those beautiful green eyes—and she has the most beautiful green eyes that I have ever seen—I just get lost in them. I have a battle going on between my head and my heart. My head says, "Slow down. Take your time. Don't rush." But my heart says, "Pull in a little closer."

The more we talk, the more I find that we have in common. Only time will tell. I don't know what the future holds, but I can only hope that Sonja will be a part of it. I find myself thinking about her all day. Here it is one in the morning, and I can't sleep. It's the first time in a long time that I haven't been able to sleep for a good reason.

I knew there would be some raised eyebrows because I was falling in love so soon after Penny's death. After all, I had been alone for only about four months. If I had been watching someone else fall in love so quickly after the death of a spouse, I might have questioned it too. But I also knew this wasn't something I had sought or planned.

I remember when I was in my twenties, shortly before I met Penny, I asked my mother, "How do you know when you've fallen in love?"

"You'll just know," she said.

Not long after that, I met Penny. After just a few dates, I told my mother, "I know what you were talking about now. Penny's the one I want to marry." We were married within the year.

I loved Penny with all my heart, and we had almost nineteen wonderful years together. I would never forget her or the boys. But Penny was gone now, and it was time for me to move on, to close one chapter of my life and begin a new one. Because I did not feel that in marrying Sonja I would be showing disrespect for Penny, I also did not believe that it was necessary to spend a certain amount of time as a single man before remarriage would be appropriate.

As for a quick courtship, with Sonja it was just like it was with Penny. It didn't take long before we both knew that we were going to get married. Late in July, I wrote in my journal,

It has been a long season of weeping and mourning, but once more joy and love have come into my life. The Bible tells us in Psalm 30:5, "Weeping may endure for a night, but joy cometh in the morning." My joy has returned, and now I can look forward to tomorrow and have a peace about my future.

I proposed to Sonja on August 10. I had originally planned to take her out for a romantic dinner and then give her a ring, but I decided against that. I'm not very good at picking out things like rings, and I wanted it to be something Sonja would like, so I wanted her to go with me to pick it out.

As it turned out, it was a Monday evening, and we were sitting on her couch, watching TV. Blake asked if he could go to his cousin's house, and Tanner wanted to go outside and play. After the boys had left, we sat there together, and I just asked her.

"Would you consider marrying me?"

I didn't have to ask twice.

We talked about dates, about when would be the best time, and at first we considered waiting another year or so, or at least until after the first anniversary of Penny's and the boys' deaths. But I didn't want to spend the holidays alone. We discussed it some more and settled on October 25.

I spoke to Erin and to Penny's parents and received their blessings. Erin cried, but she said she knew I had to move on with my life. So almost eight months after I lost my first family, God blessed me with a new one.

On Saturday, October 25, my relatives, friends, and church family gathered at Miracle Faith Baptist Church for a much happier service than the one that had taken place there eight months earlier. On that painful day I was saying good-bye to my wife and sons. My life had been shattered, and I saw no prospects for hope or happiness in my future. Now I felt as if God had restored me completely—indeed, as if He'd doubly blessed me as He did Job.

There were still many challenges ahead, but Sonja and I would face them together. The legal process was picking up steam, and in a little less than two weeks I would have to appear before Lisa Tanner and Robert Vititow to explain why I believed that Charlie Wilkinson's and Charles Waid's lives should be spared.

CHAPTER 23

FORGIVENESS

I say to you who hear, love your enemies, do good to those
who hate you, bless those who curse you, pray for those who
mistreat you. —LUKE 6:27-28

LISA TANNER and the Texas State Attorney General's office wanted to ask for the death penalty from the very beginning. In fact, they told me that if I had died that night, they would have asked for the death penalty for Charlie and Charles and for life without parole for Erin. They would have asked for the death penalty for Erin, too, if they could have, but because she was a juvenile, that was not an option.

At first, I was all for the death penalty, at least for Charlie and Charles.

They had taken Penny's, Bubba's, and Tyler's lives; they should have to pay with their own. Early on, I dreamed of helping the state carry out the death sentences. That was one of the reasons I avoided most of the court hearings related to Charlie and Charles. I didn't think I could trust myself to be in the same room with them. I could almost see myself with my hands around their throats.

But as time passed, I wasn't so sure about the death penalty.

I had always supported capital punishment. I believed that it was biblical, that God had given governments the right to take human life as punishment for crimes. I still believed that in theory. The problem was, it was no longer a theoretical issue for me. Now I literally had two lives in my hands. And although I didn't have the final word in the matter, I knew that my opinion would carry a great deal of weight.

So the death-penalty option was before me. Would I exact revenge and demand Charlie's and Charles's lives in payment for my family's?

When it came right down to it, I wasn't sure that was the right thing to do. And the more I thought about the matter, the less certain I became. My mind kept going back to the message bracelet so many people used to wear: WWJD? What would Jesus do?

Would Jesus ask for the death penalty?

As time went by and I talked with the prosecutors, I began to express some of my doubts. I hadn't decided against asking for the death penalty—yet—but I was definitely wavering.

Soon I would have to make a decision on the matter very quickly.

SNAP DECISION

I was in Princeton, Texas, making a delivery when my cell phone rang. The Rains County District Attorney's Office was calling with an urgent message. The judge had called a hearing and wanted a decision that day about whether or not to ask for the death penalty. We had to decide one way or the other, and we had to give the judge our recommendation at one o'clock.

I looked at my watch. It was 11:00 a.m. I could just barely make it to Emory in time for the hearing, but I'd have to leave right away. I called my boss at Praxair and told him I had to drive to Emory immediately for an emergency hearing. As always, he accommodated me and told me to go.

I had to push it, but I made it to the courthouse just before the hearing was to start.

Lisa Tanner and Robert Vititow met me and explained that we had to make our decision now.

I had already been wavering on the death penalty, and I didn't like having to make a snap decision.

"I'm not sure," I told them. "I've been having doubts about whether or not that's the right way to go. Why did this come up all of a sudden? Why didn't you give me some advance notice?"

They told me that the hearing had caught them by surprise, too, but they certainly had more time than they gave me. The people from the attorney general's office had come all the way from Austin. Surely they could have given me more notice. Later I wondered if they had waited until the last minute to call me because they knew I was struggling with the issue. Better to spring it on me quickly rather than give me time to think about it. I didn't know that for sure, but I certainly was suspicious.

"Look," someone said. "If we ask for the death penalty, we can always go back and change our minds. But if we refuse it now, then we're locked in. We can't change our minds. So let's ask for it now, and if you change your mind later we can go back to the judge."

That seemed reasonable to me. As long as I was able to keep my options open, I could accept their asking for death, at least for right now. I could always go back later and say I changed my mind.

It was something I would think long and hard about in the coming months.

DECIDING TO FORGIVE

The decision to forgive Charlie, Charles, and Bobbi was not easy. I had so much anger toward them stored up in my heart. I was angry not only because they took my family but because they had robbed me of everything else as well. They weren't content to stop with murder. They had to burn down my house and leave me with nothing. I resented that, and I didn't want to forgive them.

But ultimately, I forgave them because of Erin.

I had forgiven Erin only a few days after I went to Buck Files's office in Tyler and met with Lisa Tanner. As she went over all the evidence against Erin, I saw hard things, things I didn't want to believe. I was puzzled, confused, hurt. Even though I didn't want to believe Erin had been involved, it was obvious that she had been, at least to some degree. But all I knew was that she was my daughter and I loved her. On June 19, three days after that meeting, I wrote in my journal:

> No matter what happens with Erin, no matter what her involvement was, no matter what the prosecutors say, I'll always love my daughter. I'll love and support her the best way I can. . . . I thought I knew what unconditional love was, but I didn't really know till now. With unconditional love I know that forgiveness for the other three has to come. I'm not there yet, but I'm working towards that. I don't forgive the act they committed; I forgive for my own peace of mind.

My first thoughts of forgiveness were motivated by my own need. I knew that if I continued to harbor anger and resentment toward Charlie, Charles, and Bobbi, it would destroy me. I would become a bitter old man, angry at the world and unhappy with life. I didn't want to end up that way. And so I knew that even from a psychological standpoint, I needed to forgive.

But something else was at work too. I knew that I needed to forgive them because *that's what God did with me.* When I deserved no mercy, He showed me mercy by sending His Son to die in my place and to bear the penalty of my sins.

Could I do any less with Charlie, Charles, and Bobbi?

Forgiving them wouldn't mean excusing what they did. God never excused my sins. If He had, Jesus wouldn't have had to die. God gave His Son that I might have life. Forgiving Charlie, Charles, and Bobbi meant that I had to commit them into God's hands in the hope that they might come to know Him.

My forgiveness had to be complete and, as with Erin, unconditional.

If any vengeance was to be exacted on these three, it had to come from God, not from me. And that brought me back to the death penalty.

The more I thought about it, the more my mind kept going back to the phrase *What would Jesus do?* Although I didn't want to admit it at first, I knew the answer.

What did Jesus do with *me?*

I had lived for many years believing that I was a Christian, believing that I was going to heaven because I'd stepped into a baptistry that day as a young man. And yet all that time I was living in rebellion against God. After high school, when I was out on my own, I quit going to church. I started drinking and hanging out with the wrong crowd, and that went on until I married Penny. After we were married, I got back into church and even became a youth leader, but I still didn't know the Lord. I'd cleaned up on the outside, but on the inside I was still lost.

At any time during those years, God could have taken my life, and I would have gone straight to hell. I'd have been separated from Him forever because I had never trusted in Jesus Christ for my salvation.

But God, in His grace, gave me time to turn around. Time to feel the Holy Spirit making me aware of my sin. Time to feel remorse and turn to Jesus for forgiveness.

I needed to give Charlie and Charles that same time.

If they received life without parole rather than the death penalty, there was a chance that they might come to a place where they not only felt remorse for what they did but also might turn to God. Maybe, just maybe, they would place their trust in Jesus Christ, too, and be forgiven. As the hymn writer said, God's grace is "greater than all our sin," and that includes murder.

What would Jesus do? Jesus would give them time. And that's what I would do also.

I decided I would ask the district attorney and the attorney general's office to back off on requesting the death penalty for Charlie and Charles. Now all I had to do was convince them to agree with me.

MAKING MY CASE

When I spoke with Penny's parents, they agreed that we should ask the attorney general's office not to go for the death penalty. So my first step in trying to convert the prosecutors to my position was to send the attorney general's office a written request for a lighter sentence on Charlie and Charles. In a letter dated October 20, 2008, I wrote,

> *To Whom It May Concern:*
>
> *I would like first off to express my sincere gratitude to the District Attorney and Attorney General's office for your prayers and concerns during my tragic loss.*
>
> *Over the last eight months, I have had a lot of time to think and pray about the direction I would like to see all this move forward. As I reflect over the loss of my family and the pain that this has brought to my family and me, my heart tells me that there have been enough deaths. That is why I am against the death penalty and would like to see life without parole.*
>
> *I want to see them get life without parole and give them time to*

think about what they have done. I want them, in this lifetime, to have a chance for remorse and to come to a place of repentance for what they have done.

I have lost everything, my wife and two boys, and in a sense I feel I have lost my daughter as well. I have lost my home and all the years of memories from all our pictures and all the special little gifts that have been handed down over the years. Yes I have lost so much. I or my family didn't have a choice in the matter. So all I ask is for you to listen to me and my family, and grant our request.

We are the victims here, and we are hurting. We just want our voices to be heard and to be able to move on the best we can. So all I ask of you is that you listen with your heart and give a grieving family their request and a chance to move on.

Thanks so much for taking the time to listen to a grieving husband and father.

Sincerely,

Terry Caffey

Writing the letter was easy, but a letter by itself would not be enough to sway Lisa Tanner and the attorney general's office. I knew I would have to make my case to them face-to-face. We set up a meeting in Emory about a week later. The day before the meeting, I spoke with Robert Vititow.

"Is this what you really want?" he asked.

"I've had months to think about this," I replied. "This is what I want."

"Okay. You'll be meeting with the attorney general's office tomorrow. This is going to be your day to shine. You're going to have to make your case. Tomorrow is your chance. You'll have to convince them. You're asking the attorney general's office to give up the death penalty in this case, something they are dead set on having. It's not going to be an easy task. So don't hold anything back, because this will be your first and last chance to make your case."

I know Mr. Vititow was only trying to prepare me for what I would face the next day, but when I went home, I felt overwhelmed by the task ahead of me. I was going to have to face several highly trained attorneys and somehow sway them to my way of thinking. A sense of my total inadequacy for this task swept over me. I knew that if I was going to have any chance of success, it would be only through God's power.

The next day, before I went to meet with Lisa Tanner, I got on my face before God. "God, I'm going before a district attorney and two people from the attorney general's office, people who are skilled and very good at what they do. I'm just an old country boy from Alba. Will You give me the wisdom I need, the words to come out of this simple body to convince them? You say that You take the simple to confound the wise. I pray that whatever I say will just confound them. I want You to speak through me this morning. Let it be as if I'm not even there. As if it's You Yourself in there speaking."

When I got into the office with the others, I was like a different person.

We sat down at the table, and one of the first questions the prosecutors asked me was whether I was asking for a lighter sentence for the men so that they would also go lighter on Erin.

"No," I said.

"How can we be certain of that?"

"I'll tell you. I'm so sure about this that if Erin had to be sentenced to life without parole, too, in order for Charlie and Charles to be spared the death penalty, I would be willing to agree to that. Don't misunderstand me. I don't want Erin to get life without parole. But I feel so strongly about not giving the guys the death penalty, that's how far I'd be willing to go if I had to.

"They have my family's blood on their hands, but I don't want their blood on mine. I want to be able to honestly say that I gave them every opportunity to find remorse and turn to God.

"I've been praying about this for months. You can't say that this is a rash decision on my part. Y'all approached me back in March about the death penalty. Now it's October. I've woken up many nights with this on my mind. I've gotten up at two, three, four o'clock in the morning, praying for these guys who killed my family.

"One thing that has kept popping into my mind is the slogan that was popular a few years back. For some reason, every time I ask God what He would have me to do, all I can think about is WWJD? What would Jesus do?

"I believe that Jesus would give them life sentences, because He came to give life and give it more abundantly.

"When it comes time for them to die, I want that to be in God's hands, not mine. I believe if Jesus were in my place, He would spare them, even though they took my family's lives."

When the meeting was over, Lisa Tanner and the others agreed to ask for life without parole for Charlie Wilkinson and Charles Waid. Sometime later Lisa said to me, "In the meeting that morning, you had me speechless. Nobody's ever been able to do that to me. You were very convincing."

I smiled, because I hadn't been the one doing the speaking that day. It was all God.

CHAPTER 24

FACE-TO-FACE

Do not be overcome by evil, but overcome evil with good.
—ROMANS 12:21

I WAS FULL of mixed emotions on the day Charlie Wilkinson and Charles Waid were to be sentenced.[2] Although I had made the conscious decision to forgive them and had been influential in having the death penalty eliminated as a possible sentence, I still knew that I would be walking a very thin line when I sat across the table from them for a victim-offender meeting. This would be the first time I had sat face-to-face with Charlie since before the murders. I wasn't sure how I'd react when I saw him. The one thing I didn't think I could handle would be if either of those young men took what we were doing lightly, or mocked Penny and the boys. I was afraid I'd lose it.

---

[2]Charlie Wilkinson and Charles Waid were sentenced on January 6, 2009, four days after Erin Caffey and Bobbi Johnson.

Sonja and I arrived at the Rains County Courthouse a little early, and as we were getting out of the car, I gave her my keys, my wallet, my cell phone, and other personal belongings.

She gave me a strange look. "What are these for?"

"That's in case I don't come back out," I said.

"What?"

"I think I've got myself under control," I said. "But if either one of them comes in with a cocky attitude, if they so much as smirk, I'm afraid I'll jump right over that table and try to strangle them. So," I told Sonja, "I'm giving you all my things in case I get arrested while I'm in there."

We entered the courthouse, and Detective Almon met us. Sonja stayed behind while I followed the detective down a hallway to the room where I would meet with the men who had murdered my family.

Charlie and Charles, in shackles and wearing orange jumpsuits, were standing right outside the door. But they faced the wall and stood at attention, with their noses right up against the paneling.

Detective Almon led me past them and into the meeting room, which held only a table with a chair on each side.

"Mr. Caffey," he said, "I'm sorry, but I have to pat you down and make sure you're not carrying any weapons."

"It's okay," I replied. "I'd have been surprised if you didn't."

I stretched my arms out and spread my legs so he could frisk me. After he patted me down, I sat in the chair on the far side of the table. I had prepared a list of ten questions I wanted to ask Charlie and Charles. I unfolded it and laid it on the table before me.

They brought in Charles Waid first.

When he sat down across from me, he looked me in the eye, but his expression was devoid of emotion.

I looked at him and asked my first question: "Are you sorry for what you did? Do you have any remorse?"

"Of course I'm sorry for what I did," he said.

"Then you have remorse?"

"Yes."

His response was matter-of-fact, as if I were asking him about his favorite TV show instead of whether or not he felt bad for murdering three people.

I asked my second question: "If it were possible, would you have done things differently? Do you wish you hadn't done it?"

Again his answer was straight and to the point. "Of course I wish I hadn't done it, but it's too late now."

"Why did you do this? What was your motive?"

"It was money. I was promised two thousand dollars."

"What did you need two thousand dollars for?" I already knew the answer, but I wanted to hear him say it.

"I was trying to get custody of my kids, and I needed two thousand for court money. Charlie said y'all had money in the house and he'd pay me after the job was done."

I shook my head, amazed. "So, you were willing to kill children to get children? Where's the logic in that?"

"I really don't know," he said. "I can't answer that. I have kids of my own."

I moved on to the next question. "Initially, whose idea was it to kill my family?"

"Erin's," he said.

"Erin said that she tried to stop you that night when y'all got there and told y'all to leave. Is that true?"

He shook his head. "I don't think so," he said. "I don't think anyone tried to stop us."

The next questions were difficult to ask, and again I already knew the answers. But I wanted him to confront the truth about what he had done and admit it. I wanted to see his reaction when he said it. I wanted to watch his eyes and see if there was even a shred of remorse.

"Who shot Bubba, and who stabbed Tyler?"

Again, his answer was calm, direct, and matter-of-fact. If he felt any emotion or remorse, he concealed it very well. "I shot Bubba, and we both stabbed Tyler."

"If y'all wanted us dead, that was one thing," I said. "But why did you kill the kids?"

"I don't know," he said. "I don't have a good answer for that. Like I said, I have children of my own. I guess I'll just have to live with that."

"You bet you will," I replied. "For the rest of your life."

I went on. "Does it hurt or bother you that you took human life?"

"Yeah, it bothers me. Of course." From his tone, I got the impression that he considered that a stupid question.

In my last question, I wanted to address the issue of Charles's relationship to God: "When you die, do you know where you will spend eternity? Do you know Jesus as your Savior?"

Charles's answer nearly floored me. He nodded. "Yes. I know Jesus, and I'm going to heaven when I die."

I hadn't expected that response. I suppose I expected him to say either, "No, and I don't care" or "No, but I wish I did know." The thought that he might say he knew Jesus Christ and expected to go to heaven had never entered my mind.

I nodded toward the sheriff's deputy and said I was finished talking to Charles. They escorted him out, and a few seconds later brought in Charlie Wilkinson. The difference between Charlie's demeanor and Charles Waid's was like night and day. When he sat down across the table from me, he immediately looked at the floor.

"Look me in the eye, Charlie."

He looked up, and I read my first question.

"Are you sorry for what you did? Do you have any remorse?"

Charlie hung his head and looked at the floor again.

"Charlie, look at me," I said again.

When he looked up, his eyes were filled with tears.

"Yes," he said. "I'm sorry for what I did."

"So, are you remorseful?"

He nodded. "Yes."

I moved on to my next question. "If it were possible, would you have done things differently?"

Charlie dropped his gaze to the floor again. "Yes."

"Charlie, I want you to look me in the eye like a man. Tell me what you would have done differently."

"I wouldn't have done it at all," he said.

"Why did you do this? What was your motive?"

"I did it for Erin. I did it for love," he said.

I shook my head. "That's very sick love. Did you think for one instant that you were going to be able to come in and kill us, take off with my daughter, get married, live happily ever after, have a family of your own, and never have this come up or bother you? Did you ever think you'd even get away with it?"

Charlie hung his head again and shook it. "No. I wasn't thinking," he said softly.

"You've got that right," I replied. "You weren't thinking."

I moved on to my next question. "Initially, whose idea was it to kill my family?"

"It was Erin's idea from the start," he said. "It was her plan and her idea."

"I'm not buying it," I said.

Charlie didn't respond, so we went on to the next question.

"Erin said that she tried to stop you that night when y'all got there and told y'all to leave. Is that true?"

For the first time in our meeting, Charlie's demeanor changed. He got a puzzled look on his face and his tone became defensive, "No. Of course not. It was totally her idea."

My next question seemed to strike a nerve. "Who shot Bubba, and who stabbed Tyler?"

Charlie hung his head again. "Charles Waid shot Bubba and stabbed Tyler." Then he added, "But I may have stabbed a few times at Tyler, too."

"If y'all wanted us dead, that's one thing. But why did y'all kill the kids?"

"Charles Waid said we couldn't leave any witnesses."

"So you're putting all this on Charles Waid?"

He nodded, "Uh-huh."

"So you're not taking responsibility for killing my two children?"

"No, I'm not saying that," Charlie replied.

"That sounds like what you're saying. Look me in the eye, Charlie. Right now, I'm not addressing Erin. I'm not addressing Bobbi. I'm not addressing Waid. I'm addressing you. We're here. Me and you. When are you going to admit and confess and take ownership and responsibility for what you did?"

Charlie didn't answer.

"You need to be responsible for your actions and for what you did. I don't want to hear what Waid did or that it was Waid's idea. You could have run out. You could have said no, even before you came into the house. You're as guilty as Waid."

He looked down at the floor.

"Does it bother you to know that you took human lives?"

Charlie nodded, eyes still fixed on the floor.

"Do you know Jesus as your Savior? When you die, do you know where you will spend eternity?"

As Waid's had, Charlie's answer surprised me.

He looked up and rather matter-of-factly said, "Heaven."

I looked over to the guard and nodded. Our face-to-face meetings were over. Now it was time for the public hearing and my victim impact statement.

VICTIM IMPACT STATEMENT[3]

I had about a fifteen-minute break before I faced Charlie and Charles again. This time I would give my victim impact statement. After that, the two young men would be sentenced to spend the rest of their lives in prison. I already felt drained from my face-to-face meetings with them, but I would find the strength for the next few minutes. Those minutes were for Penny and Bubba and Tyler.

When I entered the courtroom, I noticed a few members of the media present, but I decided to ignore them and focus on what I was about to say. I took a seat at the prosecutor's table up front, on the left side of the courtroom. Lisa Tanner, from the attorney general's office, couldn't attend, so she sent one of her assistants to represent her. Robert Vititow, the Rains County district attorney, also sat with me.

Not long after I sat down, Charles Waid and Charlie Wilkinson were brought in and seated at the defendant's table. When the judge gave me my cue, I got up and walked to the front of the courtroom, carrying a framed photo of my family and me. Before I started, I walked over and set it on the table in front of Charlie and Charles.

"While I speak, I want you to look at this. I want you to see what you took from me." As I gave my statement, I noticed several times Charlie and Charles looking down at that picture.

I was nervous as I began to speak, but God gave me strength, and I began my statement:

> As I stand here today and look face-to-face with the ones who murdered my family, I wasn't sure how I would feel. Would I have anger, sadness, or grief of losing my family? Not sure what emotions I would have. Maybe a mixture of them all.

[3]Charles Waid and Charlie Wilkinson were sentenced in separate hearings a few minutes apart. Thus, Terry gave his victim impact statement twice, first to Charles Waid and then to Charlie Wilkinson. Because his statement was the same both times, in this book the two hearings have been combined into a single scene.

One thing is for sure. I see two troubled young men before me. Two men who have thrown their whole lives away. You've thrown your lives away, and for what? It was so senseless.

At first I had so much anger, so much bitterness towards you, but in time God has shown me what it means to forgive. So I want to say to you today, I forgive you, not so much for your sake, but for my own. I refuse to grow into a bitter old man. If I am going to heal and move on, I must find forgiveness in my heart.

That has been the hardest thing that I've ever had to do, because you have taken so much away from me. You took my wife of eighteen years, whom I'll never be able to see or talk to again. You took my boys away from me. Matthew, only thirteen years old. Tyler, only eight years old. I'll never be able to see my boys drive their first car. I'll never see them graduate high school or college. I'll never get to see my boys walk down the aisle and get married. Never will they be able to give me grandchildren. Because of you, I'll never be able to see my boys grow up.

Then, after you took my family away, you didn't stop there. You burnt our house down, taking from me all my family photos, all the little special gifts and cards, all the things that were so precious to me. You took all these things from me as if they were nothing. So for me, forgiveness hasn't come easy. But in spite of your hatred and evil efforts, I'll carry on with all the wonderful memories that will forever be ingrained in my heart. And that is something you will never be able to take from me.

You took lives and the prosecutors wanted to send you to death row, but I protested and asked them not to. You took lives, but I gave you back life in return. That's the difference between you and me. I'm not a murderer. Life to me is so precious.

So I ask you today, was it worth it to throw away your

lives? To spend forever in prison, locked away behind bars, knowing you will never get married. You will never have children. You will never have grandchildren. You will never see another sunrise or sunset as free men or walk on a sandy beach. Never ever will you enjoy the things a free man does.

So again, was it worth it?

I have been asked many times how could I forgive someone who has murdered my family and taken away the most precious thing that I had. I found that answer and my comfort in Romans chapter twelve, "Bless them which persecute you. Bless and curse not. Recompense to no man evil for evil. Provide things honest in the sight of all men. Dearly beloved, avenge not yourselves, but rather give place unto wrath: for it is written, 'Vengeance is mine; I will repay,' saith the Lord. Therefore if thine enemy hunger, feed him; if he thirsts, give him drink; for in so doing thou shalt heap coals of fire on his head. Be not overcome of evil, but overcome evil with good."

Charlie Wilkinson, may God have mercy on your soul.

Charles Waid, may God have mercy on your soul."

I picked up my picture, went back to the prosecutor's table, and sat down.

Moments later the judge asked Charlie and Charles to stand up, and then he sentenced them to spend the rest of their lives in the Texas Department of Criminal Justice, Institutional Division.

Charlie Wilkinson and Charles Waid were headed to prison for the rest of their lives. It was a better outcome than they could have expected apart from my intervention. The prosecutors told me that the only reason any of the defendants received a lighter sentence was because I asked for it.

I hoped that Charlie and Charles would use wisely the time they had been given.

CHAPTER 25

PLEA BARGAIN

Nothing is impossible with God. —LUKE 1:37 (NIV)

DESPITE MY VICTORY in persuading the attorney general's office to back off the death penalty for Charlie and Charles, I knew that another, much more difficult, negotiation lay ahead. Erin couldn't receive the death penalty, but she could be sentenced to life without the possibility of parole. And that's exactly what the attorney general's office wanted. Robert Vititow, the Rains County district attorney, believed that Erin had been involved in the crime but was not the mastermind. However, Lisa Tanner and the attorney general's office were convinced that Erin had planned and orchestrated the whole thing. They wanted her to receive the maximum possible sentence.

Because Erin had been charged with three counts of capital murder, if we went to trial, it would be an all-or-nothing proposition. Either Erin would be acquitted and go free, or she would be convicted. Conviction would mean an automatic sentence of life without parole.

I wished she were facing a lesser charge, because then a jury would have had some discretion in the sentencing.

Part of me wanted to "roll the dice" and go to trial in hopes that God might work a miracle and have Erin acquitted. The problem with that approach was that if a jury didn't render a verdict in our favor, Erin would never have any hope of getting out of prison. As I thought about the evidence and about the fact that Charlie, Charles, and Bobbi would all testify against Erin, I knew there was little chance that she would be acquitted.

Erin's attorney, Mr. McDowell, had hired a private investigator in hopes of discovering something that might work in Erin's favor, but he wasn't able to find much that would be helpful. As we moved into December, it became clear that if we went to trial on charges of capital murder, Erin would be convicted. Mr. McDowell confirmed my fears when he told me there was almost no chance of an acquittal.

It was important to me that Erin have hope. I wanted her to be able to look forward to the possibility—even if it was a remote possibility—of living on the outside again. If we lost at trial, no such hope would exist. I began to think that a plea bargain, rather than a trial, was in Erin's best interest. Would the prosecutors be willing to give us one?

This situation was completely different from those of the two men. In their case, I could make a moral argument for a lesser sentence. But that kind of argument would carry no weight this time. In fact, the prosecutors would be able to use my own words against me, if they wanted to. When I was presenting my argument about Charlie and Charles, I said that I'd be willing for Erin to face life without parole if that was the only way for the two men to escape the death penalty.

Lisa Tanner and Robert Vititow were under no obligation whatsoever to offer or accept a plea bargain. Ultimately, Erin was at their mercy. If they chose to go to trial, there was nothing I could do. I prayed that God might again give me wisdom when it came time to speak to them about a plea bargain.

As it turned out, I received an extra month to think about that question. Originally, it had looked as if Erin's trial would start in January 2009, but at a pretrial hearing early in December, Penny's mother asked if we could move the trial date off.

"With the Christmas season coming up, it would be nice to get a break from all of this," she said. "Couldn't we move it off a month?"

The prosecutors discussed it and agreed that perhaps a little break would be a good thing for everybody. The judge agreed as well. There would be another pretrial hearing in January, but the trial was moved off a month to February 2009.

I didn't know it at the time, but that pretrial hearing would quickly become much more.

BLIND SIGHT

By now I was speaking in a different church almost every Sunday, and although doing so was a great blessing, it was often tiring and stressful because the uncertainty of Erin's situation wore heavily on me. Nevertheless, I spoke whenever I could because it was one way I could see God bringing something good from my tragedy.

Sometimes when I spoke, I set a picture of my family on the pulpit or the Communion table. When it felt right, I dedicated the message to them. I didn't always do that, but I always brought the burned page with me and showed it to the congregation as part of my testimony. Even after eight months, I was still amazed by that page and how it had survived the fire.

One thing still bothered me. I didn't know what book that page had come from. Because the edges were burned, I could find no title or author name. It had almost certainly been one of Penny's books. She was the big reader in our family. Before the tragedy, I didn't read much, so I wasn't familiar with the books she had. By this time I had pretty much given up hope of finding out the name of the book or its author.

I should have known that God had that matter well in hand.

On December 7, I spoke at Greenville Bible Church in Greenville, Texas. After the service, Pastor Jim Corbet and his wife, Marcia, invited me to their home for dinner. After we finished eating, I stayed and visited a little while, and we got to talking about the page.

"I sure wish I knew what book it was from," I said. "I've been trying to figure it out for months."

"It sounds like Jim Pence's book *Blind Sight*," Jim said, and Marcia agreed.

Jim Pence was a former pastor who lived in the Greenville area and was now involved in prison ministry. He supported his ministry by writing and also by teaching a karate class for children being home-schooled. In fact, Erin and Tyler had actually been in his karate class for a couple of years, and I vaguely remembered that Jim had given Penny one of his books, although I didn't remember the title.

Pastor Corbet went to his bookshelf and got his copy of *Blind Sight*, and I went out to the car and brought back the burned page. We sat together and flipped through the pages, looking for a match. We didn't have to look very long. Near the end of the book, Pastor Corbet found the matching page. And I had my answer.

God had preserved that page from *Blind Sight* and used it to send me a message I desperately needed to hear. As I read the back cover and leafed through the book, I was even more amazed. *Blind Sight* was a novel about a man who had lost a wife and two children and was trying to understand how a good God could have allowed his family to die. Not only was the page a message *to* me, but the book could have been written *about* me.

I called Jim Pence from the Corbets' house and gave him a capsule version of my testimony. I told him that I had found a page from a book and wanted to read it to him because God had used it to turn me around. As I read the words from that burned page and explained how God had used those words to assure me of His presence with me, I heard a sound on the other end of the of the phone.

Jim was crying.

NEGOTIATING

Christmas 2008 was my first without Penny and the boys.

I knew there would be painful memories, but the holidays would have been almost unbearable if God had not blessed me with a new family. It was such a joy to sit with Sonja on Christmas morning and watch Blake and Tanner open their presents and to see the joy and delight on their faces.

But although I spent Christmas and New Year's with my new family, Erin's upcoming trial loomed like a thunderhead over everything I did. I was to go to the Rains County Courthouse on Friday, January 2, for Erin's final pretrial hearing. Jury selection would begin on February 2; the first day of testimony would begin one week later. Throughout the month of December, I had been preoccupied with thoughts of what to do about Erin. But by the time I went to the courthouse on January 2, I had come to a decision.

When I spoke to Mr. McDowell, I told him, "I'd like to seek a plea bargain for Erin." The others agreed to talk with us, and minutes later I was once again sitting across the table from experienced prosecutors, this time negotiating Erin's future as if we were haggling over the price of a new car.

Lisa Tanner was a tough negotiator. Her offer was three life sentences plus fifty years. That was essentially the same as life without parole.

I knew that Bobbi Johnson had accepted a plea deal that gave her forty years with parole eligibility in twenty. She had received a lighter sentence because although she was an accomplice, she didn't use a weapon and didn't participate in the killings. Personally, I wanted to see Erin get the same sentence that Bobbi received, but I knew the prosecutors would never agree to that.

"Look," I said. "I'm the victim here. I didn't have a choice when those two men came into my house and shot my family. I didn't have a choice when they burnt my house down. I know I don't have a choice about whether or not Erin goes to prison. Please. Give me something."

The prosecutors left the room. After some discussing, they came back with an offer of two life sentences plus fifty years.

"That's not acceptable," I said. "I want Erin to have some hope of getting out someday. I want her to have something to look forward to."

I think the prosecutors might have become a little irritated at this point, but after talking about it some more, they came back and asked, "What do you think is fair?"

"Where can I meet you halfway?" I asked. "I'd like to see Erin get what Bobbi got, but I know that's not going to happen. How about we go somewhere in between the guys and Bobbi? Two life sentences and twenty-five years." That sentence would allow Erin to become eligible for parole when she was fifty-nine years old.

There was more discussed, but finally the prosecutors agreed. Instead of having to stand trial, Erin would be allowed to plead guilty to murder and would receive two life sentences plus twenty-five years.

Lisa Tanner and the other prosecutors made sure that I understood the reason they were agreeing to a lesser sentence for Erin: "We're doing this because of you, to spare you the pain of going through a trial. All four of these young people owe you something. If you had not survived, we'd have gone for the maximum on all four of them."

Then they said, "Are you sure Erin will agree to this? We can talk about this deal all day, but if Erin doesn't sign off on it, it won't do any good."

"She'll agree," I said.

Mr. McDowell backed me up. "Erin will take whatever Mr. Caffey says. She trusts him and knows that he will get the best deal possible for her."

The prosecutors agreed and went to draw up the papers.

While they were gone, I asked Mr. McDowell, "What do you think of this deal?"

"I can't tell you what to do," he said, "but I think it's the best you're going to get. It's better than I'd have gotten if I'd taken it to court." He shook his head in amazement. "I've never seen an attorney general back down like that."

"Never underestimate the power of God," I said.

Mr. McDowell nodded. "Amen to that."

DADDY AND DAUGHTER AGAIN

Mr. McDowell and I went back to another office, and Erin was brought in. When the prosecutors returned, Mr. McDowell went over the plea deal with her and explained the terms. Erin agreed and signed the papers.

"I'm glad it's not going to trial," she said. "I don't want to put you through that. I'm ready to go start serving my sentence."

Mr. McDowell went to hand over the paperwork to the judge, and he left Erin and me alone in the office. I was a little surprised, because there were no guards or deputies with us. It was the first time since the murders that we'd been together alone.

As we sat in that little office, we began to talk. We didn't discuss the sentencing or the prospect of prison life or anything related to the case. We just talked.

We talked about shopping, her grandparents, her friends.

For about twenty minutes while we waited for her paperwork to be processed, we sat together and were just daddy and daughter again. We were practically on the edge of our seats. Over the past year we had visited, but it was always with the knowledge that our conversations might be recorded. On top of that, we had talked through a static-filled phone with a piece of Plexiglas between us, guards overseeing us, and a room full of other people who also were trying to talk.

And we were never able touch.

It didn't dawn on me until later that these twenty minutes might have been the last time Erin and I would be able to just sit together and enjoy each other's company. We relaxed, we smiled, we laughed, and we enjoyed that brief time together.

We would get to visit again when Erin went to prison, but the next time we would be able to visit alone, to sit together by ourselves and talk about whatever was on our minds, wouldn't come until I was at least eighty-four years old.

We were talking and laughing when Mr. McDowell came back and said, "The judge is ready. It's time to go out there."

STANDING WITH ERIN

Instantly the relaxed atmosphere evaporated. Erin began to cry, and so did I.

"I'm scared. I don't know what to say," Erin said through her tears. "What if the judge asks me something I don't know how to answer?"

Mr. McDowell told her not to worry. "Your response will be 'Yes, sir' and 'No, sir.' He's not going to ask you to elaborate on anything. He'll ask if you agree to these terms, and all you have to give are yes or no answers. It's all going to go very quickly," he added. "The judge will come out and ask you some questions, you'll answer yes or no, and we'll be done. If we're out there ten minutes, I'll be surprised."

"It'll be okay, Erin," I said. "I'll be right there with you." I looked over at Mr. McDowell. "Is it all right if I stand beside her?"

"Oh, by all means," he replied.

And so we went back into the courtroom for the last time. Erin stood at the defendant's table, with Mr. McDowell on her left and me on her right. As the judge handed down the sentence, I reached over and took her hand.

I stood with my daughter as she received two life sentences and twenty-five years for her involvement in the murders of her mother and two brothers. I wanted to run and hide, to find a place to cry, but I stayed by her side.

I will always stay by her side.

At that same hearing, Bobbi Johnson was also sentenced for her part in the murders. In the entire pretrial process, I never got to talk to Bobbi. The prosecutors never asked for my input about her sentence, but I did not object to the sentence she received. I thought it was fair.

When sentencing was complete for both Erin and Bobbi, the judge turned to me and said, "Mr. Caffey, is there anything you would like to say?"

"Yes, your honor," I said. "I would like to say a special thanks to Erin's lawyer for all the hard work he's done, all the time and effort he's put in. I'd like to thank the district attorney and the attorney general's office. We may not always have seen eye to eye during this process, but I want to thank you for showing my family and me dignity and respect and for listening to us and following your hearts with this. I want to thank everyone from the sheriff to the local police departments for all their efforts. I'm sorry for all the pain this may have caused some, but I want to thank you for what you've done for me, and for Penny and the boys."

After the judge had adjourned the court, Erin and I embraced one last time.

Tears flowed down our faces.

"I love you, Daddy."

"I love you, too, Erin."

Then I watched as Erin was led out of the courtroom and on to her new life.

CHAPTER 26

FACING REALITY

We know that God causes all things to work together for good to those who love God, to those who are called according to His purpose. —ROMANS 8:28

MY ALARM CLOCK RINGS about five. Saturday mornings are supposed to be times for sleeping in, but it's visiting day at the Texas Department of Criminal Justice (TDCJ), and I'm going to see Erin. She lives in Gatesville, where most of the women's prison units in Texas are located. This will be Erin's home until she is at least fifty-nine years old. I will be eighty-four when she becomes eligible for parole.

Gatesville, near Waco, is about a three-hour drive from Wills Point, so if I'm going to get there close to the time visiting hours start, I need to be on the road by five-thirty or six. Visitation at all TDCJ units runs from eight in the morning till eight in the evening on Saturdays and Sundays. I suppose I could get there later, but the three-hour drive home would make for a late evening.

Erin's unit isn't easy to find, but once you know where it is, you can't miss it. High double fences and razor wire surround the prison, and everything is a drab gray. Imposing guard towers stand at every corner.

When I arrive at the first checkpoint, I have to pop my hood and open my trunk for a visual search. While correctional officers search my car to make sure I'm not transporting any contraband, I go to a second building. There I identify myself and tell the officer that I am there to see Erin. Once she verifies my name on Erin's visitor list, she gives me a piece of paper that clears me to enter the prison.

I park my car and walk up to a double gate, called a sally port, which is unlocked remotely by an officer in either a control center or a guard tower. I step inside the first gate and close it behind me. The metal gate makes an unsettling metallic clang as it locks. Seconds later there's a buzzing sound as the inner gate unlocks. I pull it toward me and walk through. When I close the gate, I hear that clang again. I am now inside Erin's prison unit. But I'm still not through with security checks.

I follow a sidewalk to another building, where I have to remove my shoes, my belt, everything in my pockets, and any metal item I might have on me. Then I stand on a rubber mat with my arms outstretched while a male correctional officer pats me down and then "wands" me with a metal detector.

After I clear security, I go through another sally port into the visiting area, a small metal building, where I will wait for Erin to be brought in. Sometimes she comes right away. But if I have arrived during count—when the officers count the inmates to make sure everyone is still there—I can wait an hour or more. Erin will not be allowed to come out until count clears throughout the entire prison.

When she does get there, we have exactly two hours to visit. Not a minute more.

I am not allowed to bring paper money into the prison, but I am permitted to bring in enough change to buy Erin some soda and candy from the vending machines in the visiting areas. I can't bring anything to her from the outside, not even simple things like soap or toothpaste. She must buy everything through the prison commissary.

Erin enters the building from the other end, dressed in white pants and a white pullover top—the standard uniform for all TDCJ inmates. When she sees me, she smiles. It is the bright smile I had been so used to but hadn't seen for such a long time. We embrace and find an empty table.

Even her eyes are smiling now. For most of the last year, even when she did smile, her eyes told a different story—one of pain and loneliness and sorrow.

For her own protection, Erin had spent much of 2008 in administrative segregation, more commonly known as solitary confinement. As the months passed in the county jail, the twenty-three-hour-a-day solitude took its toll on her mentally and emotionally.

Now that she was out of the county and into the state prison system, her appearance and mental state had been consistently improving. Because Erin would still be a juvenile until July 2009, she was being kept away from the general prison population with three other girls about her age.

Usually Sonja comes with me when I visit Erin, but today I've come alone, and Erin knows why. It's time for us to clear the air, to discuss what went on that night. Time for me to learn what she knew and when she knew it.

It's time for both of us to face reality.

FORGIVENESS AND DENIAL

When I first learned that Erin had been involved in the attack on our family, I didn't want to believe it. What father would?

If Erin had been a delinquent or had been difficult most of her life, the knowledge might have been easier to accept. If our family members had always been at each other's throats, I might have understood what happened. If there had been abuse or violence in our house, the events of March 1, 2008, might have made sense.

But none of those things was true.

We were a happy family. We loved each other. Erin got along well with her brothers, and with us. The only signs of trouble we had were in that last year as she began to go out with boys. But although we struggled with Erin over the kinds of boys she wanted to date, neither Penny nor I had any idea that the problem was anything more than typical teenage rebellion, the kind parents across the country face every day.

So when Texas Rangers came to my hospital room and told me that Erin's involvement was "great," my world collapsed. I simply could not comprehend how that could be possible, or why it would happen.

As more evidence came to light and as I met with the Rains County district attorney and the representatives from the attorney general's office, a portrait of Erin that was totally foreign to me began to emerge. Lisa Tanner and Detective Almon portrayed Erin as a calculating mastermind who had initiated, organized, planned, and executed the murder of her family.

Through the months between Erin's certification, plea, and sentencing, I grappled with questions about my daughter's involvement, wanting to believe her because she was my daughter and because none of what I was hearing fit her personality. This was not the Erin I knew.

What had frustrated me most was my inability to ask Erin direct questions. There were so many things I wanted to know about what had happened that night. I wanted to find a way to reconcile the prosecutors' accusations with the loving daughter I had known for sixteen years. But because the case was ongoing and the judge had issued a gag order, those questions were off-limits.

So from March 2008 to January 2009, when Erin was sentenced, I was left largely in the dark. I heard the prosecution's case against Erin but heard very little of Erin's side of the story. I knew only that I couldn't comprehend how she could even have been involved in the murder of her mother and brothers, let alone how she could have masterminded the crimes. Even in the early months of 2009, as Erin was being processed and assigned to a TDCJ unit, we didn't have much opportunity to talk, and when we did, I didn't probe very deep. Each time I saw Erin, I asked her only one or two questions about what happened because I didn't want our visits to feel like an interrogation.

But now that the books were closed, so to speak, it was time to clear the air and address the hard issues. I'm not talking about the question of guilt or innocence. Long ago I had accepted the fact that Erin had some knowledge of, and therefore involvement in, the murders. What I couldn't believe is that she was the mastermind and driving force behind the crimes.

The media portrayal of Charlie, Charles, and Bobbi as reluctant participants whom Erin had persuaded to kill her family was completely unbelievable to me. I'd never met Charles Waid or Bobbi Johnson, and I had no knowledge of them. But Charlie had been in my house. I saw how he dominated and controlled Erin, how he always had to know where she was and what she was doing. I saw how angry Charlie was when we took Erin's cell phone away from her for a while. I witnessed the changes in Erin after she started back to public school and was with Charlie every day. I could believe that Erin was influenced; I couldn't believe that she was the influencer.

But even if I was wrong, no matter what she had known or what she had done, I intended to stand by her. I forgave Erin, just as I forgave Charlie, Charles, and Bobbi, and nothing would ever change that.

When I began to do interviews with the media about the case, many people misinterpreted my support of Erin and my belief that she had not been the mastermind. They saw me as a grieving father who was desperately clinging to my daughter because she was all I had left. They often concluded that I was ignoring the evidence and living in denial. It's true that I greatly feared losing Erin and hoped that somehow God would work a miracle and restore her to me. But even then I wasn't unaware of the evidence. There are entries in my journal where I say as much.

On June 16, the day I met with Lisa Tanner in Tyler, I wrote:

> I just want all the court issues to go away so that I can deal with the loss of my family. Even though Erin is still alive, I feel as though I have lost her as well. From what I am seeing as far as the evidence goes, it doesn't look good for her. I keep praying that God will perform a miracle and all will go in our favor. All the lawyers and prosecutors are saying she is going away for a long time, and that scares me so much.

But although I hoped and prayed that somehow God might give me my daughter back, those prayers didn't grow out of a denial of the situation. Rather, they grew out of a deep conviction that nothing is impossible for God.

In the Old Testament, when King David's baby lay sick and dying, David fasted and prayed and mourned before the Lord, asking that God might deliver the child. When the baby died, David's servants were afraid to tell him because they thought he might harm himself. But to their utter surprise, when they finally told him about the baby's death, David got up, washed, and asked for food. The servants couldn't believe what they were seeing. But David told them, "While the child was still alive, I fasted and wept; for I said, 'Who knows, the LORD may be gracious to me, that the child may live.' But now he has died; why should I fast? Can I bring him back again? I will go to him, but he will not return to me" (2 Samuel 12:22-23).

As Erin awaited trial and we went through court hearing after court hearing, I prayed for her release, reasoning as David did, *Who knows, the Lord may be gracious to Erin and me and perform a miracle.* That did not happen, but my praying for it to happen did not constitute denial.

Erin has been slow to reveal details of what happened that night, perhaps because she fears losing me and my love. Throughout those first few months, I often thought that she was all I had left in the world; alone in prison, perhaps she feels that I am all she has left. One thing that Erin consistently writes in all her letters to me is, "I love you, Daddy." I love her, too, and I always will.

I have forgiven Erin completely, and even if I were to learn a few months down the road that all the allegations against her were true, it would not change a thing. My forgiveness of my daughter is not partial, nor is it based on half-truths or denial. The Scriptures tell me that I must forgive others the same way God forgave me (see Colossians 3:13). God knew everything there was to know about me, saw my sin laid bare before Him, and yet He gave His Son, Jesus, to die in my place. He not only forgave all my sins; He also paid the price necessary to make that forgiveness possible.

How could I do any less than that with Erin?

Nevertheless, as we moved forward, it would be important that our relationship be based on honesty. Erin's counselor had told her that it was time she told me the whole truth. And so we met on that bright, sunny Saturday to revisit the darkest night of both of our lives.

ERIN'S STORY[4]

"Was it really your idea to kill us?" I asked.

Erin shook her head. "We were both really angry that you and Mama wouldn't let us be together. We talked for more than a month about running away together, but I kept saying that it wouldn't do

---

[4]This section is a composite of several conversations between Terry and Erin.

any good because y'all would just come after me. Charlie said that he could keep you from coming to get me, and I said, 'Oh yeah? How would you do that?' That's when he told me that he had a friend who would help him kill y'all if we paid him. I said, 'I don't know, that's crazy. Let me think about it; there's too much going on.' We thought about it and talked about it, even at school. It was just my way of venting because you didn't like Charlie, but it was like a game to me."

"What happened that night?" I asked her.

"The plan was to run away. I kept calling him because I wanted to meet him down the road. But at the last minute I changed my mind and decided not to run away. That's why I left my bag in the house when I went out to meet them.

"When they pulled up, they said 'Hurry up. Get in.' Charlie was really mad because I didn't have my bag, so we drove around for a while, drinking and trying to decide what to do. First, Charlie said he'd sneak in and get my bag and we'd just run away. But Charles Waid said, 'I came to kill, and I want my money.'

"Charlie and Charles kept going back and forth about whether or not to do it. It was like a game. It didn't seem real. Finally I got tired of them arguing and said, 'Fine. Just go do it.'"

I looked at her and said, "So you knew what they were going in there to do?"

Erin's eyes filled with tears, and she nodded.

"They said that you were talking about how awesome it was after the fact, and that you wanted to go in and see the bodies. Is that true?"

"No," she said. "Bobbi and I were both crying. Charlie and Charles were the ones who came out high-fiving and talking about how great it was. I didn't even know how Mama and the boys died."

"The prosecutors told me. Would you like to know?" I asked.

Erin's voice was quiet. "Yes."

"They shot Mama in the head. Later they came back and cut her throat. I don't know why they didn't do that to me, too. Maybe they thought I was already dead.

"Bubba was trying to fight Charlie off and keep him from hurting him and Tyler. Waid came up the stairs behind Charlie and shot Bubba in the head too.

Erin was fighting to keep control of herself. "What did they do to Tyler?"

"Tyler was hiding in the back corner of your closet. Waid stabbed him from behind. Then Charlie took his turn. It was like they were stabbing a rag doll."

Erin broke down and sobbed.

When she regained her composure, I pursued some other questions.

"When I met with Lisa Tanner, she said that you'd asked another boy to kill us before you and Charlie discussed it. Did you do that?"

She shook her head. "I told him I hated you and that I was mad at you. I never mentioned wanting y'all dead."

"When they came to get you, who quieted Max?"

"When I went out, Max was nowhere in sight. Buddy [Tyler's chocolate Lab puppy] came up to me, and I held him and petted him until they came."[5]

"What about your travel bag?" I asked. "Why did they throw it in the creek?"

Erin looked puzzled. "I don't know. I'd like to know that myself."

We talked a while longer, and before I knew it, our two hours were up. I hugged Erin and watched as she went back through the door toward her new home. I made my way back through the sally ports and gates, back to my car.

WALK IN MY SHOES

I believe Erin. Nevertheless, there are still unanswered questions between us. One of those is, who quieted Max, our black Lab mix?

---

[5]Max survived the attack and was adoped by a local family.

Max barked at everything. I had heard him bark earlier, but he didn't make a peep during the attacks. Someone had kept him quiet.

Other questions disturb me too. Once when we visited Erin, she said that she had a great life with Penny, the boys, and me. She said that we were the greatest parents and that she did not live a sheltered life, as some members of the media reported. But if that's so, how could she go down such a bad road, go behind our backs, drinking and having sex? How could she let someone like Charlie tear down what her mother and I had spent sixteen years building? The only answer I can come up with is that we are all sinners, and our enemy Satan is alive and well and attacking the family. He still prowls around like a roaring lion, looking for someone to devour (see 1 Peter 5:8).

There are still other questions and gaps in the story that I have not yet been able to fill in. For those, I give Erin the benefit of the doubt. Perhaps she doesn't remember; perhaps she's not yet ready to talk. I do not believe that my daughter is innocent, but until I receive undeniable proof to the contrary—or she tells me so herself—I will not believe that she masterminded the murder of her mother and brothers. And if people take my willingness to accept my daughter's word over the word of two admitted child killers as proof that I'm in denial, then so be it.

When I decided to tell my story publicly, it was because I believed that it could benefit others. But the public reaction to some of the media pieces has taken me by surprise. Most people were encouraging and supportive, but some online posts cut so deeply that for a time I regretted the decision to allow the media to tell this story. In fact, I was so discouraged that for a time, I was ready to give up on ministry altogether.

Not only have I been accused of being in denial about Erin, but some have even said that there must have been something wrong with our family: Penny and I were abusive, or Erin was too sheltered because she was homeschooled, or a number of other suggestions too unkind to print here. Some criticized me for leaving my burning house too quickly, suggesting that I didn't do everything in my power to save my family. A few have concluded that I must not have loved Penny and the boys very much because I remarried so soon after their deaths. Others have predicted that my new marriage won't last. Still others have suggested that I am trying to profit from my family's tragedy by writing a book about the murders.

In response to those who judge me, I recall something Bubba wrote in his journal less than two months before he died. On January 10, 2008, he wrote, "To me, the Native American proverb, 'Never criticize a man until you've walked a mile in his moccasins,' means don't judge somebody by the way they may appear."

I've written this book so that people may, in a small way at least, walk in my shoes. Writing about the murders and what followed has been a painful experience. In the process, I've had to relive many things that I would rather not have thought about again. I've reopened a lot of wounds that only recently had begun to heal. I would never want anyone to have to live through a tragedy such as mine. But if by reading this book, people can see God's goodness and faithfulness, then it will have been worthwhile.

If you were to ask me what I have learned through all of this, I could summarize it in one simple sentence. Ironically, it's a sentence that inmates of every race and color chant in prison chapels across the United States: "God is good, all the time. All the time, God is good."

In the midst of horrific tragedy: God is good, all the time.

When all seems lost: God is good, all the time.

When nothing in life makes sense: God is good, all the time.

When our pain seems too great to bear: God is good, all the time.

When our world is spinning out of control: God is good, all the time.

And because God is good all the time, we can press forward and go on with life. We can continue to serve Him because even when we don't understand the circumstances, we know that the God and Father of our Lord Jesus Christ is Lord of the circumstances. We know that He is sovereign, He is in control, and He is good: "We know that God causes all things to work together for good to those who love God, to those who are called according to His purpose (Romans 8:28).

All the time, God is good.

THE SOUNDS OF HOME

IT'S DIFFICULT TO PUT into words how much my life changed in less than a year. If it were a vessel, in 2008 it went from full to empty, empty to shattered, shattered to restored, restored to full, and finally, full to overflowing. At the end of the book of Job, God restores Job and doubles his wealth. As I look back on all that has happened, I feel that I have likewise been doubly blessed. I am not wealthy by any means, at least not materially. But the Lord has poured out blessing upon blessing over this past year.

It's interesting that when God restored Job, He gave him twice as much material wealth as before. But He gave him the same number of children Job had at the beginning of the book: seven sons and three daughters. I used to wonder why the Lord didn't double the size of Job's family.

But as I thought about it, I realized that He did—because Job never lost his first family. Not really. They were dead, but they were with the Lord. So when God gave Job seven more sons and three more daughters, his family doubled. And I imagine that now they are gathered around God's throne as one large family.

Even though I have remarried, Penny, Bubba, and Tyler will always be a part of my life. They have gone on to be with the Lord, but they are far from dead. Often I recall the words Brother Todd spoke at their funeral: "Penny, Bubba, and Tyler are more alive right now than they were when they were here with us." That's true. And I look forward to the day when we'll all be together again. I don't know if there are musical instruments in heaven, but if there are, you can be sure that Penny will be at the piano. Bubba will have a harmonica and a guitar. As for Tyler, well, he'll probably be looking for a puddle to jump in or a rope to swing on.

I still go out to the cemetery to visit them. Recently Sonja and I found a small bronze statue, about a foot tall, of a little boy and his dog, riding in a little wagon. The boy and dog are both wearing floppy hats and goggles. It reminded me so much of Tyler and his chocolate Lab puppy. He would put that puppy in his wagon and pull him all around the yard. We bought the statue and took it out to the cemetery along with a few Hot Wheels cars for Tyler's tenth birthday. Sometimes I just have to marvel at God's providence in arranging a resting place for my family so near to where I would be living when I married Sonja.[6] Even before I fell in love with her, the Lord was working behind the scenes.

As much as I loved my first family, I am also thankful that God brought Sonja, Blake, and Tanner into my life. As He did with Job, God has doubled my family. I lost a wife and two sons, and He has given me back a wife and two sons. Blake and Tanner remind me

---

[6]Terry sold his property shortly after marrying Sonja. He also sold the RV in which he had been living.

so much of Bubba and Tyler that it's almost spooky. At my darkest moments, I never imagined that I would have the joy of raising a family again and watching two sons grow up. But God has done it. He has restored me completely.

God didn't need to give me another daughter, because Erin is still with me. Our situation is different, and it will be many years before we have even the possibility of being together in an unstructured, unsupervised environment. Nevertheless, Erin is here, and she is part of my new family. When I visit her, Sonja goes with me. Sometimes Blake does too. Tanner will have to wait until he's seventeen (TDCJ rules).

We are thankful for the time we can have together.

There's one thing that is different about my relationship to my new family. I take nothing for granted. Before this tragedy, I took little notice of the mundane things of life, the things that happen every day. The sound of Penny's dryer creaking and clinking at bedtime because she forgot to start the load earlier. The sound of Bubba and Tyler arguing over a TV program or some other unimportant thing. The sound of Erin talking on the phone and giggling with a girlfriend long after she should have gone to bed.

In the past, I didn't pay much attention to these things.

Now, that's different. Through all that has happened, I've learned to savor life, and I try to extract the last ounce of joy and delight from every moment. I've learned not to take anything for granted because I know that it can all be gone in an instant. I take in every sight, every sound, and I enjoy them all—even those mundane things.

A clinky dishwasher.

Two boys arguing over the remote control.

They're the most beautiful sounds in the world.

The sounds of home.

TERRY'S JOURNAL

AT THE SUGGESTION of his counselor, Terry began keeping a journal of his feelings during the months of his recovery. He started making journal entries early in June 2008 and continued to the end of July. The entries cover the period of time from the day Terry moved back to his property until shortly after he fell in love with Sonja.

This journal is, in part, the source material for chapters 20 through 24. We have included Terry's journal as an appendix because it gives a more complete picture of his internal struggles and growth after he found the page from *Blind Sight*. The entries have undergone light editing in the interest of clarity, but they are substantially as Terry wrote them.

JUNE 7, 2008 – 7:30 A.M.

Today I woke up with both excitement and fear, for today after three months and seven days I am going home. Maybe not home as I once knew it, but I'll be moving my RV onto my land. I have such a sense of peace to go home, but yet my heart races with fear and anticipation as I move forward, not knowing what lies ahead. Will I have a peace and a joy to be back where my family once was, with all the wonderful memories? Or will fear take over and will I be able to stay there? So many questions race through my mind this morning as the anticipation floods my soul. Only time will tell. So today is a big step forward for me. So today I lean on God and Psalm 71:16, "I will go in the strength of the Lord."

Well, it's 9:50 p.m. and, oh, what a day it has been. Tommy and I finally got my RV moved to our land. Even though it was just moving it up the road, it felt as if I was off on a long journey. As I drove in my truck behind Tommy as he pulled my RV with his tractor, I felt my heart begin to race, and I had both excitement and fear at the same time. It was a new chapter in my life. This was a new beginning. I was finally stepping out on my own, but I felt God leading all the way.

As my RV trailer turned up the long drive for the first time, I said out loud, and it was probably good that I was alone, for one would have thought that I was crazy and had lost my mind. I said, "Penny. Kids. We're home." It felt as if I was bringing part of them back.

I could see in my mind Penny standing in the doorway as she did often as I would pull up the drive, home from work. I could see Bubba out back shooting aluminum cans off the fence row. I could see Tyler outside playing with his little red wagon full of dirt, and more dirt on him than in the wagon. I could see Erin coming out to greet me, "Hi, Daddy. How was your day?" So, yes, it felt as if I was coming home.

Only time will tell if staying here is good. But for now, I'm halfway there but not quite home yet. I will never be completely home until God calls me home to be with Him and my family, to see Penny and the kids, to see my Daddy and precious Mama, and all my grandparents and loved ones [who have] gone on before.

Well, it's way past 10:00 p.m. I must get some rest, for tomorrow is another big day. I've got to preach in Brookston, TX, and it will also be Bubba's birthday. He would have been fourteen. So tonight I ask for God's grace and protection as I spend my first night completely alone.

So for tomorrow's challenges, I rest again upon Psalm 71:16, "I will go on in the strength of the Lord."

JUNE 8, 2008 – 7:40 A.M.

Well, I made it through the first night on my own here on our land. At first I had a little trouble going to sleep, for every sound that echoed through the night would cause me to get up and look out the window. Though after a little talk with God and turning it over to Him, I began to slip away into a deep sleep, for the long day had finally caught up with me.

The hardest thing for me to be alone now is the quietness all around. I miss my family so much. I miss the sounds of home. Just the simple things like the dryer belt squeaking as Penny would put on a load of laundry just before bed. I would ask her, "Why do you wait until we go to bed to start the dryer?" She would say in her soft, sweet voice, "I'm sorry. I just forgot to earlier."

I miss the sounds of the kids upstairs at night as they would giggle and whisper, and I would say to the boys, "You need to be quiet and go to sleep." I miss Penny lying next to me in our bed as we would hold one another and drift off to sleep. Still to this day I will often wake up in the middle of the night, forgetting that she is not there and reach out my arm, only to find an empty place there. I miss my friend, my lover. I miss my wife. I just miss my family.

Today is Bubba's birthday. He would have been fourteen. He

was such a sweet boy with a good heart. He loved everyone, and it showed by his kind spirit.

So I face another day, trying to move forward the best that I can, just putting my trust in God. Well, it's time to stop and get ready to go. Have to go speak at Brookston Baptist Church.

It's 9:05 p.m. Sunday, and oh what a day it has been. So full of emotions, both happy and sad. Happy because I had a blessed time in the Lord, being able to preach God's Word and give my testimony. God is so good, and He gives me strength that I couldn't get on my own.

Today was also a sad day. Today was Bubba's birthday. Instead of planning a birthday party for him, I spent some time at the cemetery, thinking we should be together as a family celebrating his birthday. So instead, I grieve today, alone, with my family gone. The emptiness that is left inside can't even be put into words.

In the past three months I have gone through several firsts: Tyler's birthday, Mother's Day, Easter, Memorial Day, and today Bubba's birthday. Then there comes Father's Day next Sunday. Only by God's grace have I made it this far, and only by God's grace will I be able to keep going. As I sit alone in my travel trailer, I can't keep the tears back, thinking of all of our family memories and all the great times we had.

I can't help but to get angry at times. I even had a little fit today. I couldn't get a shirt to go on a hanger like I wanted, and through my frustrations of the day I just began to throw hangers as I cried out to God. "It just isn't fair. I want my family back, and I need them." And I asked God, "How can I go on without them?"

Even though I have experienced God working in my life and through others, it still doesn't change the fact that my family is gone and the grief is still there. So tonight as I try to drift off to sleep, I'll think back on all our wonderful memories together, and for now say good night.

JUNE 9, 2008 – 10:53 P.M.

Today has been one of the hardest days during my grief process. Just when I think there are no more tears, I have a day like today and they begin to flow again. I talked to Erin's lawyer today, and it looks like they are going to certify her as an adult. That scares me so much. She is only sixteen, just a child who will soon face an adult world in an adult jail. I feel like it would [be] like throwing a kitten into a den of wolves. She is not even prepared to face life on the outside, much less life in prison. I try to put it in God's hand, but being a human as I am, I still find myself worrying about it all.

Today for the first time since the early days of my grief, I had thoughts of suicide again. I thought those feelings had already passed. I guess the reality of losing Erin after I have already lost Penny and the boys is at times too much to grasp. She is all I have left, and I feel that I'm losing her as well.

As grief flooded my heart and soul as I drove home from work, I was compelled to stop by Penny's parents' house. I began to share and open up with them how great the grief has taken over. We all had a good cry, and we stood together in their living room and prayed to God for His grace and mercy. It always amazes me what a good cry can do. I felt a burden had been lifted, knowing that this wasn't over yet, but my strength had been renewed.

Penny's parents are so wonderful, and I shared with them my love for their daughter. I told them they raised a wonderful daughter and a man couldn't ask for a better wife and our kids couldn't ask for a better mom.

I want to feel normal again. The sadness and depression is something I'm not used to. I have to believe that God has everything under control and that there will be joy again. Just as the sun began to set tonight and a gentle rain began to fall on the metal roof of my RV, I opened the door with the screen pulled and just sat there. For the first time I sat quietly and listened to the birds as they chirped and felt the gentle breeze on my face as it flowed through the trailer. I realized that even though my family is gone, the sun still rises and it sets. The stars still shine, and the birds still sing. Life of all forms is so special to me now, and one thing I have come to realize is that life should never be taken for granted. We need to embrace it and live each day as if it were our last. I will cherish the memories of those who have gone on ahead, and tell those that I still have in my life that I love them, never taking them for granted. For life is a gift from God. A gift that should never be taken for granted.

Must get some sleep. Work comes early in the morning.

God, give me peace tonight.

JUNE 12, 2008 – 7:00 A.M.

Well, it's been a few days since I've written. There has been so much going on. I'm having a problem with depression this week. Seems like it all started on Bubba's birthday. I've had so much anxiety lately. I think I worry about Erin so much, knowing there is nothing I can do to help her. I just pray that God's will be done. It's all in His hands now.

Today will be another hard day. They are releasing the items that were taken that night. I have to go to the sheriff's office, and that's where they are holding the other three. I also have to go to the probation office and pick up my court summons for Erin's court date. They want to certify her as an adult. I'm just not ready for that. She is just a child. I just wish all of this was over.

Tuesday I arrived home at around 10:30 p.m. Rodney, a good friend of mine that I've known for over twenty years, took me out to dinner, and we talked for hours. Rodney has been such a good friend, just like a brother. He lays down his life, leaving his family to help me. Don't know what I would do without him.

Like I said, I returned back to my RV at 10:30 p.m. It was so dark out here in the woods, when I pulled up, I couldn't get out of my truck. Fear took over. What was I thinking, moving back to the place where my family was murdered? I drove off as quickly as I drove up, and drove down to Tommy and Helen's house, my neighbors, but they were gone. I forgot that they had left town the day before.

I said to myself, "I have to get ahold of myself." So I drove back to my place. Again, too terrified to get out, I drive off again. I drove to Bro. Wayne's house, a former pastor of mine who lived just up the road, but no one was home. So I just drove around praying that God would give me courage to return home. Finally after an hour of driving, I said, "God, I have to go home. I have to get some rest. I can't drive around all night." I drove back to my RV and said, "God help me." So I got out and came in—very quickly, though.

Once I got inside I was fine—well, once I went through my nightly ritual.

I will come in and lock the door behind me, scan my small RV, go to the bathroom and open the door. Look behind the shower curtain, then look on the other side of the bed. After doing this, I was fine.

I asked Bro. Todd, my pastor, if he would come over and pray over my land and ask God to bless it and remove all fear from me, and to put a hedge of protection all around. So I go on trusting God. I believe God will give me the peace that I need.

I mentioned earlier that my depression has really been hard this week. When I was on my way to church for Wednesday night Bible study, I asked God to speak peace, to give me a sign, send someone or something to let me know that He is still there. When I arrived at church, Bro. Todd handed me a large envelope. Inside were six cards from all over, from people that I didn't even know.

After all this time, people are still praying. They still care. I believe that was my sign from heaven. I couldn't hold back the tears. God had just spoken.

JUNE 13, 2008 – 8:45 P.M.

Well, today has been a very good day if you compare today with the rest of the week. It's like I'll start doing really well, then something will happen and depression will set in. Today has been a lot better. I've been talking to God a lot lately, and I have some wonderful friends that care so much. They are so good about calling or stopping by.

Tonight, Bro. Wayne and Diane stopped by and took me out to eat. They are so wonderful. . . . Even though Bro. Wayne is [my] ex-pastor, I still look up to him as my pastor in so many ways. He and Diane came that night when all this happened. They arrived before the ambulance or sheriff's office did. They have always been there and are willing to help in any way. Last night I was still having a little trouble with depression and couldn't sleep, so they asked me to spend the night. Wayne and I stayed up late and talked while Diane and their son Justin went to bed. It was so good to just sit and talk to an old friend.

One thing that I have learned while going through the grief process is to surround yourself with family and friends. Isolation is the worst thing to do while you are grieving or going through depression. Finding people that can relate to how you feel also seems to help. So many will say—and they mean well—"I know how you must feel." But in reality they can't totally understand unless they have walked where you have.

I found a support group, Grieving Forward. Susan and her husband Harvey are such sweet people. They lost their son several years back, and after a long road back to recovery they started a support group. The love in that room was so real and comforting,

knowing we all had one thing in common—we all had lost someone whom we loved so dearly. So I look forward to returning next
month, being with my new friends.

Gotta sign off for now.

JUNE 15, 2008 – 9:30 P.M.

What a day, so full of emotions. It's Father's Day, and I was able to
talk to Erin tonight on the phone. That was the highlight of my
day, even if it was for five minutes. It was so good to hear her voice
once more. I have said so often, the one thing that would hurt the
most would be to take my children away. I could have lost my job,
my home, all my money, take all my worldly possessions, but to
have my children taken away is the hardest thing to deal with. So
today has been a day of unbearable sorrow and grief, but I'll always
hold the memories so close to my heart.

Well, I was able to go spend the night with Rodney, Sherrie,
and Chelsea, and then go to church with them on Sunday. What
a great time we had. It seemed to help to get away, even if just for
a couple of days. They have been such a blessing in my life. They
go the extra mile to help me get through the tough times. They
are such a good example of what a Christian should be. I just hope
that I am able to express my gratitude to them.

Saturday, Rodney and I want to the Bass Pro Shop and then
came back to his house and watched golf. I really don't like golf
that much, but you know that was one of the best times that I had
in a long time. I guess because of the fellowship and time to just
relax.

It seems that my life is so busy lately, with work, working on
my land, preaching, meeting with lawyers, and just worrying
about Erin. It's enough to wear you down. So just going, sitting,
and relaxing was just what I needed.

Sherrie and Chelsea cooked dinner last night. Oh what a meal it was. We had pork chops, mashed potatoes, green beans, and gravy. They sure can cook. Then we had lunch today with Sherrie's dad, his friend Trudy, Sherrie's brother J.C., Jonathan and his wife, and we can't forget their wienie dog, Oscar. Just being with them made my first Father's Day alone a little easier to cope with.

I left their house about 4:00 p.m. to head back home, but I had to stop at the cemetery and tell Penny and the boys that I miss and love them very much. It's a hard thing to do, to go visit the grave of your wife and two young sons. It's something that no one should have to go through.

I always thought that I would go first, and they would bury me. Never thought that I would lose my entire family in one night and be all alone at the age of 41. Erin is all that I have left, and I will stand by her side no matter what. I know she needs me, and I need her. I believe that God saved my life that night for a reason, and one of those reasons is to be here for her. I couldn't imagine her going through this without anyone, so I stand by her side and pray every day.

There's a lot of questions that I have about that night, and some of those questions may never be answered in this lifetime. One thing that I do believe, is that Erin loved her family and wouldn't want us dead. I believe they came that night, and things went bad very fast and she had no control. So I keep trusting God to see us through and in the end that He will get the victory and that His will be done.

Gotta go for now.

JUNE 16, 2008 – 9:45 P.M.

Today was another one of those hard days that seemed as if it would never end. Just when you think it couldn't get any harder, then it seems here comes another tidal wave. I had to drive to Tyler this afternoon to meet with my lawyer, Mr. Files, and the attorney general's office. Today they laid all the evidence out on the table, and it was so hard to listen to. So painful that I can't even write it down at this time. I'll just hold on to what I have heard today, and try for the next few days to let it all sink in.

I know it is still a long road ahead, and it will probably get harder before it gets any better. It has been hard trying to mourn the loss of Penny and the boys, and then have to deal with everything on Erin's side, worrying about her and not knowing what will happen to her. Then there is the other three that are locked up, not knowing when their trials will start. There is just so much ahead, sometimes it's more than I can bear. I just want all the court issues to go away so that I can deal with the loss of my family.

Even though Erin is still alive, I feel as though I have lost her as well. From what I am seeing as far as the evidence goes, it doesn't look good for her. I keep praying that God will perform a miracle and all will go to our favor. All the lawyers and prosecutors are saying she is going away for a long time, and that scares me so much.

I have lost everything that meant the most to me here on this earth. I lost my dad, and then one week later I lost my wife and two sons. Then it doesn't stop there. After taking away the most precious things to me, they then burn our house down, destroying every family photo, all the sweet little things the kids have made over the years, forever gone. Nothing left but the memories, and at times that is all I have.

I got so scared the other night because I forgot what Penny and the boys' voices sounded like. No matter what, I will never forget the love that we all shared, all the great times we had as a family. I think about all the vacations to Arkansas, the fishing trips, all the family outings. I remember all the weekends we would drive around looking for yard sales. Oh, what a time we had. I have lost everything and maybe even Erin, but I will always cherish the memories that we all had.

I just don't understand what went wrong. This kind of thing isn't supposed to happen. If only I could have seen it coming. I love my family so much, and it was my job to protect them. Penny always called me her hero, and after all this I didn't feel like one. After all, isn't a husband and father supposed to protect his family. I feel at times that I have let them down.

One thing I can say for sure is that I loved my family and they loved me. No matter what has been taken, the love and memories we all shared can never be taken away. I will always cherish what we had, and thank God for the time we had. I will never forget what took place that awful night, but I can say that all the good things in our lives sure outweigh the bad.

So, God, I ask you for strength and guidance to get through each day, and that is how I will make it. One day at a time. One foot in front of the other. Only by the grace of God have I made it this far, and by His grace He will see me through. I wonder how people who have no faith or trust in God make it through the hardships of life. I can't understand, because even as a Christian, trying to cope and trust God is still hard.

Through this journey I can feel the presence of God, leading and directing me down the path I should go. I believe God is going to bring me out of this and because of the hardships, God will make me strong. Those things that were meant to kill us will make us stronger. Thank you, God, for getting me through this day. I keep expecting great things to come of all this.

JUNE 19, 2008 – 9:30 P.M.

Today was one of my better days. Things seemed to flow in a way that brought me peace. It all started when I opened my letter from Erin this morning. She said so many things in that letter that just lifted me up. She said she loves me and her mother and her brothers as well. She also said that no matter what happens or where she ends up, that she will never forget her upbringing. She said that we did a good job raising her and the boys, and that none of this was my or her mother's fault. Because of her bad choice in a boyfriend, she feels somewhat responsible.

No matter what happens with Erin, no matter what her involvement was, no matter what the prosecutors say, I'll always love my daughter. I'll love and support her the best way I can. Erin will always be daddy's little girl. I just hope she knows how much I love her.

I thought I knew what unconditional love was, but until now I really didn't know. With unconditional love, I know that forgiveness for the other three has to come. I'm not there yet, but I am working towards that. I don't forgive the act they committed. I forgive for my own peace of mind.

Well, tomorrow is Friday, and Rodney and Sherrie have invited me to go fishing with them. I hope I can find time to go.

Time to sign off.

JUNE 22, 2008 – 4:15 P.M.

Well, it's Sunday and it's been a few days since I've been able to write. It's amazing how busy my life has become, between work, visiting Erin, and along with church, going to preach and just spending what little time I have with family and friends. I guess it helps to stay busy. It keeps my mind off everything. It's like I go out of my way to stay busy. I am getting so tired and fatigued.

I did get to go fishing with Rodney and Sherrie. I had a great time. Just being able to get away from the everyday rat race was great. They are so amazing to include me in their lives like they do. Rodney and Sherrie are so easy to talk to. I guess because they don't put on a front. They are just good honest people, and I love them so much. It's been an all around good day today and I thank God for it. My days are so up and down, so when I have a good day like today, I just thank God for it.

I preached at Roxton Baptist Church this morning, and we had a great time in the Lord today. I can still see God moving and working in Erin and my lives. God has been blessing so much. Five young people got saved at a church just up the road. I know there are many souls that will join my family in heaven someday. I don't know what tomorrow will bring. It may be one of those hard days, but for today, I thank God for it.

JUNE 23, 2008 – 10:15 P.M.

It's getting late, but I just had to take out a few moments to write. It's been a long day, with work and then revival this week. I pray for revival in my heart, to pull me closer to God. I will have a chance to preach Friday night. I always look forward to sharing God's Word, and He has been speaking to my heart tonight.

As I was turning in for the night, I went to the Lord in prayer. I prayed for Erin and for God to work in our lives on Wednesday. That will be a big day for us in court, and as the time draws near to that day, my heart fills with so many emotions. As I prayed tonight, I remembered back to one Friday night when Erin was a baby.

It was after I got off work. We were to go out to eat with Penny's parents that night. As Penny was getting ready I remember holding Erin in my arms. She was so tiny, just about six weeks old. As I held her while rocking her in the rocking chair, I remember looking down at her precious little face as she slept in my arms. Tears began to roll down my cheeks as I thanked God for the wonderful gift that He had given us. I also remember saying to her that I love you and no matter what or how big you get, you will always be daddy's little girl. At that moment I made a promise that no matter what, I would always be her daddy and I will always be there for her. Never dreamed that nearly seventeen years later I would be standing by her side while she sits in jail awaiting trial for murder. After all these years, I stand firm and true to that promise. She will

987 7　

always be daddy's little girl and no matter what, I will always be there for her. As I lay my head down tonight, and as I fall to sleep, I say goodnight to the only one that I have left, and to the one I love so dearly.

Goodnight to daddy's little girl.

JUNE 27, 2008 – 12:00 A.M.

It has been a while since I have written. My life has been so busy lately. As I sit here and ponder back on my life, I can only say, wow, what a journey it has been. I have so many wonderful memories to look back on, and I guess when I focus and draw my attention to the wonderful things in my life, it helps to drown out all the negative things that have happened.

I sit here and reflect back on my old life, and I have so many joyful occasions I can go to in my memory. I often think of Penny and the boys, and can't help but worry about Erin. I know in time God will have His will and way. I never want to forget my past or those things that I hold so dear to my heart, but I know I must move on. There is a chapter in my life that I now must close, and a new one must begin. I have often sat and wondered what my new life will be like, or will God send me a mate that I can love and share my life with. Only time will tell, but I now see a brighter future ahead, and my heart races with anticipation as I look for a new horizon.

Just when I thought I would never see over the horizon, or be able to share another beautiful sunset with a woman, or look into a woman's eyes and look deep into her soul or feel the soft touch of her hands. Just when I needed that the most, God sent Sonja. She is such an amazing person. She makes me smile and feel so warm inside. I feel as if I've known her for years and that I can talk to her about anything. It is so refreshing to meet someone who you can just be yourself around.

I'm looking forward to seeing her tomorrow. She has invited me to a picnic/family reunion. I'm so excited to get to know her better, to just sit and talk and share our thoughts and feelings. I am so blessed to have met her, and I feel that I have a friend that I can trust. I am trying to take it slow, but in just a short time of being around her, I feel my heart giving in. She makes me feel so good, and when I look into those beautiful green eyes—and she has the most beautiful green eyes that I have ever seen—I just get lost in them.

I have a battle going on between my head and my heart. My head says, "Slow down and take your time. Don't rush." But my heart says, "Pull in a little closer." The more we talk, the more I find that we have in common; only time will tell. I don't know what the future holds, but I can only hope that Sonja will be part of it.

I find myself thinking about her all day. Here it is 1:00 a.m. and I can't sleep. It's the first time in a long time that I haven't been able to sleep for a good reason. So as I sign off, I can only thank God for blessings that He has sent my way, and one of those blessings is Sonja coming into my life. So as I go to sleep, I somehow wish I could kiss her on the cheek, tuck her in, and say good night and sweet dreams. So since we're apart, maybe somehow she'll find me in her dreams and those dreams will carry her to a peaceful place in her mind. And as she dreams, she will know that I am there nearby.

So good night and sweet dreams.

JULY 28, 2008 – 9:10 P.M.

It has been about a month since I have written, but life has been so busy and full lately. So much has taken place over the last month. Penny's birthday has come and gone, so has Erin's.

Yesterday was Sunday, July 27th, Erin's birthday. I went to Paris to preach and share my testimony. It was so hard to go at first because my heart was so heavy for Erin. This was the first time in seventeen years that I didn't get to see her on her birthday. It seems like yesterday that we were bringing her home from the hospital after she was born. Now she is seventeen and sitting in jail for what could be a really long time. So I try to move on, but at times the journey gets so hard.

Yesterday a man came up to me after I preached and shared with me that he had lost his seventeen-year-old son on February 9th of this year. As I looked up to this six foot, six inch, larger than life man, all we could do was hug and cry together and share one another's grief. When we parted ways, it made me realize why I was there and what my calling is. Just being able to help someone along life's way, and just to be able to sit and cry with someone over their grief makes going forward for me a little easier.

There have been some positive things that have taken place over the last month. I wrote about Sonja and how I was falling for her. Well, I have fallen in love with her. She is just an amazing woman, and she brings so much joy into my life. Her two boys, Blake and Tanner, I have fallen in love with them also. They are such a joy to be around, and I believe they like me as well.

I never thought that I could fall in love again, but I have, and what a great feeling it is to be in love and to have someone love you. I was trying so hard to move slowly, but she just does some-thing to me that makes my heart race when I think of her. I think of her all the time. Sonja is always there in my mind. I think of her when I awake. I think of her when I sleep. And I think of her all day long. Even in my dreams, there she is. I now know that she is the one. I'll marry her someday, and we will start a new life together. Me, Sonja, and the boys. What a great time it will be, starting over again. A new start and a new life.

It has been a long season of weeping and mourning, but once

more joy and love have come into my life. The Bible tells us in Psalm 30:5, "Weeping may endure for a night, but joy cometh in the morning." My joy has returned and now I can look forward to tomorrow and have a peace about my future.

Well, it's getting late, so I'll sign off for now, hoping I will have a restful night and dream about Sonja, the love of my life.

TERRY'S VICTIM IMPACT STATEMENT

AS I STAND HERE TODAY and look face-to-face with the one who has murdered my family, I wasn't sure how I would feel. Would I have anger, sadness, or grief of losing my family? Not sure what emotions I would have. Maybe a mixture of them all.

One thing is for sure: I see a troubled young man before me who has thrown his whole life away. You've thrown your life away, and for what? It was so senseless.

At first I had so much anger, so much bitterness towards you, but in time God has shown me what it means to forgive. So I want to say to you today, I forgive you, not so much for your sake, but for my own. I refuse to grow into a bitter old man. If I am going to heal and move on, I must find forgiveness in my heart.

That has been the hardest thing that I've ever had to do, because you have taken so much away from me. You took my wife of eighteen years, whom I'll never be able to see or talk to again. You took my boys away from me. Matthew, only thirteen years old. Tyler, only eight years old. I'll never be able to see my boys drive their first car. I'll never see them graduate high school or college. I'll never get to see my boys walk down the aisle and get married. Never will they be able to give me grandchildren. Because of you, I'll never be able to see my boys grow up.

Then, after you took my family away, you didn't stop there. You burnt our house down, taking from me all my family photos, all the little special gifts and cards, all the things that were so precious to me. You took all these things from me as if they were nothing. So for me, forgiveness hasn't come easy. But in spite of your hatred and evil efforts, I'll carry on with all the wonderful memories that will forever be ingrained in my heart. And that is something you will never be able to take from me.

You took lives and the prosecutors wanted to send you to death row, but I protested and asked them not to. You took lives, but I gave you back life in return. That's the difference between you and me. I'm not a murderer. Life to me is so precious.

So I ask you today, was it worth it to throw away your life? To spend forever in prison, locked away behind bars, knowing you will never get married. You will never have children. You will never have grandchildren. You will never see another sunrise or sunset or walk on a sandy beach. Never ever will you enjoy the things a free man does.

So again, was it worth it?

I have been asked many times how could I forgive someone who has murdered my family and that has taken away the most precious thing that I had. I found that answer and my comfort in Romans chapter 12, "Bless them which persecute you. Bless and curse not. Recompense to no man evil for evil. Provide things honest in the sight of all men. Dearly beloved, avenge not yourselves, but rather give place unto wrath: for it is written, 'Vengeance is mine; I will repay,' saith the Lord. Therefore if thine enemy hunger, feed him; if he thirsts, give him drink; for in so doing thou shalt heap coals of fire on his head. Be not overcome of evil, but overcome evil with good."

Charlie Wilkinson, may God have mercy on your soul.

Charles Waid, may God have mercy on your soul.

TERRY'S LETTER
REGARDING THE
DEATH PENALTY

FOLLOWING IS THE TEXT of the letter that Terry sent to the Texas State Attorney General's office, requesting that Charlie Wilkinson and Charles Waid not receive the death penalty.

DATE: 10/20/08

To Whom It May Concern:

I would like first off to express my sincere gratitude to the District Attorney and Attorney General's office for your prayers and concerns during my tragic loss.

    Over the last eight months, I have had a lot of time to think and pray about the direction I would like to see all this move forward. As I reflect over the loss of my family and the pain that this has brought to my family and me, my heart tells me that there have been enough deaths. That is why I am against the death penalty and would like to see life without parole.

I want to see them get life without parole and give them time to think about what they have done. I want them, in this lifetime, to have a chance for remorse and to come to a place of repentance for what they have done.

I have lost everything, my wife, and two boys, and in a sense I feel I have lost my daughter as well. I have lost my home and all the years of memories from all our pictures and all the special little gifts that have been handed down over the years. Yes I have lost so much. I or my family didn't have a choice in the matter. So all I ask is for you to listen to me and my family, and grant our request.

We are the victims here, and we are hurting. We just want our voices to be heard and to be able to move on the best we can. So all I ask of you is that you listen with your heart and give a grieving family their request and a chance to move on.

Thanks so much for taking the time to listen to a grieving husband and father.

Sincerely,

Terry Caffey

About the Authors

Terry Caffey lives in Wills Point, Texas, with his wife, Sonja, and their two sons, Blake and Tanner. Since the tragic loss of his first wife, Penny, and their sons, Matthew and Tyler, he has gone into full-time ministry, speaking and reaching out to others who have suffered unspeakable tragedy and sharing his personal message of God's faithfulness. Terry continues to visit his daughter, Erin, regularly and remains steadfast in his belief that she did not mastermind the plot to kill his family.

James H. Pence is a full-time professional writer, editor, and Web designer living near Dallas, Texas. James came to know the Caffey family when Terry's daughter, Erin, and her youngest brother, Tyler, enrolled in James's "Karate for Homeschoolers" class. Through the karate class, James came to know both Terry and Penny. He later gave Penny a copy of his novel *Blind Sight*, the source of the mysterious scorched page that Terry found in the aftermath of the fire and that he credits with turning his life around following the loss of his family.